AIR CAMPAIGN

# PHILIPPINES 1941–42

America's disastrous start to the Pacific War

MARK LARDAS | ILLUSTRATED BY GARETH HECTOR

OSPREY PUBLISHING
Bloomsbury Publishing Plc
Kemp House, Chawley Park, Cumnor Hill, Oxford OX2 9PH, UK
Bloomsbury Publishing Ireland Limited,
29 Earlsfort Terrace, Dublin 2, D02 AY28, Ireland
1359 Broadway, 12th Floor, New York, NY 10018, USA
E-mail: info@ospreypublishing.com
www.ospreypublishing.com

OSPREY is a trademark of Osprey Publishing Ltd

First published in Great Britain in 2026



A catalog record for this book is available from the British Library.

ISBN: PB 9781472870865; eBook: 9781472870872; ePDF: 9781472870889; XML: 9781472870858

26 27 28 29 30 10 9 8 7 6 5 4 3 2 1

Maps and diagrams by www.bounford.com
3D BEVs by Paul Kime
Index by Mark Swift
Typeset by Lumina Datamatics Ltd
Printed by Repro India Ltd.

Title page: see caption on p.83.

**Author's acknowledgment**
I'd like to thank the staff of the Pearsall Public Library and the Helen Hall Public Library for getting me research materials I needed for this book.

**Author's note**

This book describes events that occurred in the middle of the 20th century, from the early 1930s to the mid-1940s. The world was a different place then, with different attitudes, different boundaries (political and cultural) and very often, different names. I have used the period names in this book along with the political divisions of that era. The most profound differences are in today's Taiwan, which was then the Japanese vassal province of Formosa, with Japanese names for its cities and geographic features. Similarly, I report period attitudes as they existed, not as we wish they would be.

I use the term Commonwealth of the Philippines troops rather than referring to them as allies. At the time the Philippines were still part of the US. Their forces had the same status as US National Guard units in other US colonies (including Puerto Rico). They were part of the US Army since, in July and August 1941, their armed forces were "nationalized," inducted into the US Army, and under command of Washington, D.C. rather than the Commonwealth Government.

The Allies code-named all Japanese aircraft, rather than use Imperial Japanese names and identifiers for these aircraft (except for the A6M, the famous Zero). This Allied naming system was introduced in mid-1942, after the end of the Philippine campaign. Their use during the period of the Japanese invasion of the Philippines is anachronistic. However, they were commonly used in postwar Allied accounts, so have been listed in the aircraft section.

The Japanese Army and Navy used different naming systems for their units:

Imperial Army Air Service:
*Hikoshidan* Air Division
*Hikodan* Command
*Sentai* Regiment
*Chutai* Squadron

Imperial Navy Air Service
*Koku Kantai* Group
*Koku Sentai* Division
*Kokutai* Squadron

**Abbreviations**

The following abbreviations indicate the sources of the illustrations used in this volume:

AC – Author's Collection
LOC – Library of Congress, Washington, D.C.
NARA – National Archives
NMAF – National Museum of the US Air Force
USNHHC – United States Navy History and Heritage Command
Other sources are listed in full.

**Author's dedication**

To Clark Summers: soldier, scholar, and fellow Ricochetti.

# CONTENTS

# INTRODUCTION

Despite being the permanent Army airfield closest to Japanese-held Luzon, Clark Field was home to the USAAF's longest-ranged bomber, the B-17. It had the best maintenance facilities of any Philippine airfield, and the complex four-engine bombers required constant servicing and maintenance. (AC)

For ground crews at Clark Field on December 8, 1941 it was a typical Philippine Monday. Many were hung over, brought on by too much drinking the previous night. Most had been in the Philippines less than a year, brought over by a buildup that began soon after 1941 started and accelerated throughout the year. In the last two weeks, there had been war warnings, and the temptation to party hard to relieve strain and boredom was constant. Most hoped for a quiet Monday.

That changed as dawn broke. Around 0200hrs Philippine time, the Imperial Japanese Navy bombed Pearl Harbor in Hawaii. Unofficial word of the attack and the presumed state of war with Imperial Japan arrived in the Philippines by 0330hrs. Official notification reached Manila by 0500hrs.

Yet US reaction was slowed by a case of the Mondays. While General Lewis Brereton, commanding Army Air Forces in the Philippines, wanted to launch airstrikes against Japanese-held Formosa, he could not get permission to do so. General Richard Sutherland, chief of staff to Douglas MacArthur, supreme commander in the Philippines, would not grant permission until he cleared it with MacArthur, and MacArthur was still unavailable early Monday morning.

Frustrated, Brereton in Manila called Clark Field at 0800hrs, and ordered all aircraft airborne. He did not want his aircraft caught on the ground. The ground crews and air crews scrambled, hastily preparing the B-17s there to launch.

Soon the ground crews fueled the B-17s, hangover and all, then watched them fly off. Many had not been bombed up. They were not supposed to fly anywhere in particular, just bore holes in the sky away from Clark. The important thing, they were told, was to get them off Clark Field before the Japanese arrived.

They were followed by Clark's Pursuit Squadron, the 20th. Their P-40Bs has sped off buzzing like angry hornets, streaking to intercept Japanese bombers reported flying south over Lingayen Bay. Another set of P-40s, probably P-40Es from one of the two squadrons at Nichols, could be seen in the sky north of Clark. They were probably covering the airfield.

Then . . . nothing. The next few hours were filled with rumors and little else. The Japanese had landed at Lingayen. A massive Japanese fleet was off Manila Bay trading shots with the forts there. Saboteurs had set Manila afire. The Japanese hadn't really bombed Hawaii – this was all an elaborate drill. The Japanese had not only bombed Hawaii, they had landed troops there. It was all nonsense, the typical garbage filling the air when no one knew anything. Yet every soldier at Clark Field believed that whatever happened it was going to be a quick war, the American Eagle would quickly change the Rising Sun to the Setting Sun.

One thing everyone at Clark Field knew: they were at war with Japan. Those were real bombs loaded onto the big bombers; 300lb and 600lb demolition bombs, not 100lb practice bombs. And real .50cal ammunition belted into the B-17s guns, complete with tracers. They were burning fuel at rates forbidden in peacetime, and the officers were running around like agitated ants. This was no drill.

Yet some enlisted at Clark remained sure it was a drill. Nothing was happening. One B-17 was still held on the ground for a recon flight over Formosa. The brass did not want to send the Fortresses up there blind. Some at Clark Field felt aviation gasoline would be better spent delivering bombs to the Japs than boring holes in the sky.

Then the B-17s returned to Clark Field after a long morning airborne. To speed refueling they were parked wingtip to wingtip. The ground crews were servicing them, rearming, and refueling them, turning them around for a fresh launch. The Fortress crews were in the mess hall, having lunch.

The P-40s had returned, too. The squadron from Nichols landed, refueled, and was already back in the air, headed south. The Japs were supposed to be heading for Corregidor. The Clark Warhawks had also just landed. They saw Japanese bombers, but those bombers were headed north. The fighters left them alone. They were likely a diversionary force. They had seen no other aircraft so they returned home, low on fuel. Now they were lining up on the runway to start their midday patrol.

Suddenly the air raid siren sounded. Looking up they saw more aircraft in the sky than they had ever seen together before. They were in a tight, picture-perfect formation, three groups of nine-aircraft formations, with the nine aircraft in three three-bomber "Vs." Those on the ground counted 27 in all, in a massive V of Vs. A second, identical formation behind them. There was also a swarm of things that looked like hornets behind and below the bombers.

The antiaircraft batteries opened up, but the Japanese bombers were too high. A lot of shells appeared to be duds. The ones that did go off exploded well below the formation. Then, as the formation approached the airfield, they saw black specks separate from the aircraft. Bombs. They had to be.

Many stood and gaped at the spectacle above them, some ran for cover. There were no bomb shelters or even slit trenches. It had been peacetime yesterday and either would have marred the pristine surface of the airfield. The closest thing to cover was either open ground or a few muddy, shallow drainage ditches. Wise soldiers ignored the mess mud made of their uniforms, and threw themselves flat into ditches.

Suddenly the earth around Clark Field shook as explosives went off, continuing to shake with the thunder of exploding bombs for well over a

Clark Field (shown in this 1938 photograph) was the largest US airbase in the Philippines when the war started. It was also the oldest. Located in the Luzon Plain, it was designated as the section of Fort Stotsenburg for use of the Signal Aviation Section shortly after Fort Stotsenburg was established in 1903. (AC)

minute. When there was a lull, survivors could see bombs had cratered the runway, catching the P-40s on their take-off runs. Maybe the first few had gotten off the ground before the bombs landed, but the rest had not. Those who had stood watching were now bloody bundles of rags, lying on the ground. The second wave of bombers swept in, and the earth shook again as their bombs hit the airfield's buildings. The mess hall collapsed trapping those inside.

Then enemy fighters swept in. They hammered every aircraft on the ground. They chewed the gasoline-filled B-17s apart, igniting the gasoline in their formerly filled, now leaking, fuel tanks. They crisscrossed the airfield, firing first at the aircraft, then at anyone moving on the ground, then at the buildings.

Some men ripped .50cal machine guns out of the wrecked P-40s and B-17s, to throw them on improvised mounts and shoot back. Those men did little to damage the Japanese, but gained the satisfaction of knowing they had fought back. Finally, the shooting stopped as the Japanese planes flew away.

When it was over the formerly proud aircraft of the Far East Air Force at Clark Field were twisted scrap metal. Few looked salvageable. The runway was cratered, although a bulldozer could quickly fill in the holes. It would not be paved at those spots, although maybe some crushed stone with a roller could fix that. The hangar and workshops were smashed. So was the mess hall. The barracks seemed okay.

Yet even as the Japanese departed, repair efforts were beginning. Fires were being doused at the burning buildings, debris was getting cleared, and useful items salvaged. The maintenance staff began working on the damaged aircraft. The Japanese were probably done for the day. Even if they were not, the war was just beginning. The US Army Air Forces needed as many of the damaged aircraft on Clark Field repaired and flyable as possible.

Because of its size and importance, Clark Field was an obvious and high-priority target for Japan if it wanted the Philippines. It was hit on the war's opening day by a major air raid. This is a Japanese painting of the attack. (AC)

Every additional aircraft available would help even the odds against the Japanese. A few of those at Clark Field that day began to realize they had underestimated the Japanese. That maybe the war would not be as quick as everyone thought that morning. Or nearly as easy.

It was the opening day of a campaign that would be decisively decided within a month's time, but would linger for five more months after that. It was a campaign illustrating textbook coordination between Japanese land, sea, and air forces. It was also a campaign illustrating the inadequacies of strategic bombing concepts in an environment where tactical doctrine dominated.

The Japanese demonstrated how to do it right, using techniques the V Air Force, successor to the defeated FEAF, would emulate in its march across the Pacific back to the Philippines. The US demonstrated the mere presence of heavy bombers, even when you committed over a third of your available force, did not lead to victory unless they were paired with relevant tactical deployment. The Philippine campaign of 1941–42 was more than the first air campaign between Imperial Japan and the United States. It became the model for all subsequent land-sea-air campaigns between the two for the rest of the Pacific War.

# CHRONOLOGY

## 1937

**July 7** Second Sino-Japanese War begins.

## 1940

**September 22–26** Japan occupies Tonkin and northern French Indochina.

**September 27** Japan signs the Tripartite Pact with Germany and Italy.

**October 16** US President Franklin Roosevelt imposes an embargo of scrap iron and steel to Japan in retaliation for Japan's occupation of Tonkin.

**November 27–December 15** Japan flies photoreconnaissance missions over Luzon.

**December 9** France and Japan sign a treaty allowing Japanese forces to occupy all of French Indochina.

## 1941

**May 6** Two new fighter squadrons (P-40s) and one new bomber squadron (B-18s) become operational in the Philippines.

**July 26** Roosevelt embargoes petroleum sales to Japan and freezes Japanese assets in the United States after Japanese troops occupy all French Indochina.

**August** FEAF disperses warplane squadrons to alternate airfields.

**September** 50 P-40s sent to the Philippines.

**September** Nine B-17s fly from California to the Philippines.

**November** Two P-35 fighter squadrons are activated in the Philippines.

**November 3** General Lewis Brereton arrives in the Philippines to take command of the Far Eastern Air Force.

**November 6** Japan activates its war plans, starting operations leading to war.

**December 1** Patrol Wing 10 is activated in the Philippines.

**December 4** Japanese aircraft begin familiarization flights over the South China Sea and Luzon Straits.

In 1939 the US air garrison in the Philippines was small and obsolete. By early 1941, when these aircraft participated in maneuvers there, it had upgraded to inadequate and obsolescent with the addition of P-35 (foreground) and B-18s (background). More was needed. (USNHHC)

**December 8** Japan attacks the US Pacific Fleet in Pearl Harbor, and launches concurrent attacks on British, Dutch, and US holdings in the Far East, including the Philippines.

Japanese land on Batan Island to set up air base.

Japanese carrier aircraft attack seaplane carrier *William B. Preston* and its seaplanes at Davao Harbor.

Japanese aircraft attack Iba and Clark Fields, doing heavy damage to both.

**December 10** Japanese land at Aparri and Vigan.

Japanese aircraft attack Del Carmen, Nielson, and Nichols Fields, doing heavy damage at all.

Japanese aircraft hit and destroy Cavite Naval Yard.

US aircraft attack Japanese shipping off Aparri and Vigan on multiple raids.

**December 11** US Navy abandons Cavite.

Cavite, in Manila Bay was the US Navy's biggest naval base in the Far East. Disabling it was a high priority for Japan. On December 10, 1941, the Imperial Navy launched a massive airstrike against Cavite. This Japanese painting shows their view of the attack. (AC)

**December 12** Over 100 Japanese bombers strike multiple airfields throughout Luzon. Zeros strafe and destroy all PBYs at Olongapo.

Japanese land at Legaspi, capturing the airfield there.

**December 14** B-17s from Del Monte attack Japanese at Legaspi.

**December 15** Patrol Wing 10 departs the Philippines.

**December 17–20** B-17s are withdrawn from Del Monte to Batchelor Field.

**December 20** Japanese land at Davao, Mindanao, capturing its airfield.

**December 22** Japanese main force lands at Lingayen Bay.

**December 23** B-17s from Australia bomb Japanese shipping at Davao and Lingayen Bay.

**December 24** Japanese land at Lamon Bay, east of Manila, flanking US defensive lines.

**December 25** Japanese land on Jolo to set up a naval air base.

Retreat to Bataan Peninsula ordered for US forces.

**December 26** Manila declared an open city.

**December 29** Japan begins week-long aerial bombardment of Corregidor.

### 1942

**January 2** Manila is occupied by Japan.

**January 2–6** Japanese launch daily air raids against Corregidor.

**January 4** US fighters from Bataan attempt to intercept Japanese bombers attacking Bataan.

**January 5** B-17s from Australia bomb shipping in Davao Harbor, staging through Del Monte.

**January 7** Japan withdraws all Imperial Navy aircraft and most Imperial Army aircraft from the Philippines.

**January 9** B-17s from Kendari bomb shipping in Davao Harbor, staging through Del Monte.

**January 10** B-17s from Malang bomb Jolo.

**January 26** US fighters from Bataan attack Japanese-held Nielson and Nichols Fields.

**February 1–2** US Fighters strafe and bomb barges supporting a Japanese landing on the southern end of Bataan.

**March 2** US Fighters from Bataan attack Japanese shipping in Subic Bay. Four P-40s are lost.

**March 16–17** MacArthur and his staff are evacuated to Australia by B-17 from Del Monte.

**March 20** Japan reinforce their air forces in the Philippines with 60 Ki-24s, 24 G4Ms, 12 A6Ms and 12 Navy dive bombers.

**March 24** Japan opens second aerial bombardment campaign against Corregidor. It continues until 6 April.

**March 26** Three B-17s from Australia evacuate Philippine President Quezon, senior Philippine government officials and their families to Australia from Del Monte Field.

**April 6–7** Japanese break US lines at Bataan. Surviving US fighters fly to Mindanao.

**April 7–12** B-17s from Australia stage to Mindanao, attacking Legaspi, Iloilo, Cebu and Davao. US fighters strafe Davao.

**April 9** US resistance on Bataan ceases.

**May 1** Japanese capture Del Monte and Lake Lanao, ending US air operations in the Philippines.

**May 7** Corregidor falls to Japanese invasion. US forces throughout the Philippines are ordered to surrender.

# ATTACKER'S CAPABILITIES

The Ki-51 (later code-named "Sonia" by the Allies) was typical of the light bombers and dive bombers used by the Imperial Army. Although it entered production in 1939, it had fixed landing gear to improve rough field performance. (Wikipedia)

The air campaign supporting Japan's 1941 invasion of the Philippines involved two principal units: the Imperial Japanese Army (IJA) Air Force's 5th Hikoshidan (Air Division) and the Imperial Japanese Navy (IJN) Air Force's 21st and 23rd Koku Sentai (Naval Air Flotilla) of its 11th Koku Kantai (Naval Air Fleet). It was a rare example of Imperial Army and Navy cooperation. Most Japanese air forces attacking the Philippines were based in Formosa (today's Taiwan) a long-held Japanese colony.

While the Japanese had extensive infrastructure in Formosa, its air forces were mostly made up of aircraft capable of operating on primitive or improvised airfields. Their fixed landing gear aircraft could easily operate off grass or dirt airfields, and they had ground support units that were mobile and could quickly move to new airfields and provide basic logistical and field maintenance support.

The Japanese Imperial Army and Navy had independent and parallel aircraft, infrastructure facilities, organizational names and weapons systems. The two services were bitter rivals, exhibiting almost as much enmity to each other as to their real enemies. Even with the same sized bombs or gun calibers, they used different designs. In some cases, they could not be shared with the other service. The Army and Navy .30cal machine guns chambered different

With fixed landing gear and rifle-caliber machine guns, the K-27 was inferior to the P-40 and even P-35 in everything but maneuverability. Yet it was the primary fighter aircraft of the Imperial Army's 5th Hikoshidan, the air division used in the Philippines. (AC)

types of rounds, which could not be reliably exchanged. Even in the one instance where they shared an aircraft design (the Mitsubishi Ki-15/C5M) the aircraft had different engines for Army and Navy versions.

Nor did they typically share bases, facilities, or intelligence. When they did so, it was with great reluctance, generally due to intervention of the Emperor. This manifested itself in many ways over the course of the war, and during this campaign. It meant Japan, the second smallest of what were then the world's six greatest powers, maintained two sets of aircraft, facilities, and weapons.

## Aircraft

Except for its two main bombers, the Ki-21 and Ki-48, the aircraft of the 5th Hikoshidan were the oldest in the Imperial Army inventory. Many were verging on obsolescence. That did not prevent them from being effective in an environment where Japan ruled the skies. These included the:

**Nakajima Ki-27 (Type 97 Fighter, Allied Code-name Nate):** Designed in 1935 and first flown in 1936, the Ki-27 was the standard Imperial Japanese Army fighter in the late 1930s. The Ki-27 was the last fixed landing gear fighter fielded by the Imperial Army. It had all-metal construction, a closed cockpit, and a low wing. By 1941 it was being phased out, replaced by the Nakajima Ki-43 *Hayabusa*. The 5th Hikoshidan continued flying it through the Philippine campaign.

Highly maneuverable, it was powered by a 780hp Nakajima Ha-1 Kotobuki Otsu (Ha-1b) 9-cylinder air-cooled radial piston engine, which gave it a top speed of 290mph (470km/h) and a cruising speed of 220mph (350km/h). It was short-legged with a combat range of 627km (390 miles). With a gross weight of 3,946lb (1,790kg), it was armed with one 12.7mm Ho-103 machine gun and one 7.7mm Type 89 machine gun. It could carry four 25kg (55lb) bombs or two 130l (34gal) drop tanks. Inferior to the P-40, it was equal to or better than other US fighters in the Philippines. Thirty-six 5th Hikoshidan Ki-27s participated in this campaign.

**Mitsubishi Ki-21 (Sally):** The IJA's standard heavy bomber when the Pacific War started, it was the heaviest bomber in the IJA inventory in 1941. It belonged to the first generation of all-metal, retractable-landing gear Japanese warplanes. It entered production in 1938, remaining the Army's first-line bomber throughout the war.

Its maximum speed was 268mph (432km/h) at 4,000m (13,125ft), its service ceiling 28,215ft (8,600m), and standard combat range carrying a 750kg bombload of 1,500km (932 miles). It was powered by two 850hp 14-cylinder air-cooled Nakajima Ha-5 KAI radial engines. The Ki-21 had a single 7.7mm Type 89 machine gun in flexible hand-held mounts in the nose, dorsal, ventral positions, and one on either beam. It was recognizable by a long dorsal greenhouse, housing a hand-held machine gun. It had a crew of five: pilot, co-pilot, navigator/bombardier, radio operator/gunner, and gunner. It had a maximum bombload of 1,000kg (2,250lb). There were 18 5th Hikoshidan Ki-21s in this campaign.

**Mitsubishi Ki-30 (Ann):** First flown in 1937, it was a low-wing, fixed-gear, all-metal, single-engine light bomber. It had an enclosed cockpit and a crew of two. At the end of its operational life in 1941, the Philippine campaign saw its last combat use. Even there, it was committed only after Japan achieved air supremacy.

It had an 850hp 14-cylinder air-cooled dual-radial engine. Its maximum speed was 263mph (423km/h), its cruise speed 240mph (380km/h), and a range of 1,700km (1,100 miles). It had a crew of two (pilot and gunner), carried a 440kg (882lb) bombload, and was armed with one fixed, forward-firing 7.7mm Type 89 machine gun in the wing and a flexibly-mounted 7.7mm Type 89. Its ceiling was 28,120ft (8,579m). The 5th Hikoshidan used 33 Ki-30s in this campaign.

**Kawasaki Ki-48 (Lily):** The IJA's standard light bomber in 1941–42, it entered production in July 1940. The Ki-48's normal bombload was 300kg (661lb), its maximum speed 298mph (480km/h), its service ceiling 31,170ft (9,500m), and its range 1,980km (1,230 miles). The Ki-48, an all-metal monoplane, had retractable landing gear and an enclosed cockpit.

It had two 14-cylinder 950Hp radial, air-cooled Nakajima Ha-25 engines, and a crew of four: pilot, navigator/bombardier, radio operator/gunner, and gunner. It was armed with three machine guns: single hand-held, flexible 7.7mm Type 89 machine guns mounted nose, ventral and dorsal positions. The Ki-48 had no protection for the crew or fuel tanks, depending on speed and maneuverability for safety. While one of the fastest bombers when it first appeared, fighters reached its speed by 1941. The 5th Hikoshidan fielded 27 Ki-48s in this campaign.

**Mitsubishi Ki-51 (Sonia):** The replacement for the Ki-30, introduced in 1939, it was another all-metal, low wing, fixed-gear, single-engine bomber. Smaller, better armed and protected than the Ki-30, it carried a smaller bombload and served as a ground-attack aircraft and dive bomber. It was used extensively in the Philippine campaign.

With a 950hp 14-cylinder air-cooled Mitsubishi Ha-26-II dual-row radial engine, its maximum speed was 263mph (423km/h), its cruise speed 240mph (380km/h), and its range 1,060km (660 miles). It had a crew of two (pilot and gunner), carried a 200kg (440lb) bombload, and had two fixed, forward-firing 7.7mm Type 89 machine guns in the wing and a flexibly-mounted 7.7mm Type 89. Its ceiling was 27,130ft (8,270m). Thirteen Ki-51s participated in this campaign.

**Mitsubishi Ki-15 and C5M (Babs):** A reconnaissance aircraft used by both the Imperial Army (Ki-15) and Navy (C5M), it began as a civilian fast mail plane in 1936. Entering service in the Imperial Army in 1937 as an attack bomber, the Imperial Navy adopted it the following year as a reconnaissance aircraft. By 1940 both services used it as a reconnaissance aircraft. A low-wing, single-engine monoplane with fixed landing gear, it had an aluminum structure and fabric covering.

Army and Navy versions used different engines. Late-model Ki-15s had a 14-cylinder air-cooled Mitsubishi Ha-26-II dual-row radial engine with 900hp. The C5M2 used a Nakajima Sakae 12 12-cylinder air-cooled engine producing 950hp. Top speed was 300mph (480km/h) with a cruising speed of 200mph (320km/h) and a range of 2,400km (1,500 miles). Ceiling was 37,400ft (11,400m). Both had a crew of two, and were armed with a single aft flexible 7.7mm machine gun and could carry 250kg (550lb) of bombs.

While the 5th Hikoshidan aircraft used in the Philippines were verging on obsolescence, the 11th Koku Kantai aircraft present used what proved to be the dominant designs of the first two years of the Pacific War. They were the aircraft most often encountered by US and

The Imperial Navy's G4M was its premier long-range strike aircraft. Along with the Mitsubishi G3M it was used in its land-based *rikko* units. Although an excellent bomb platform it was completely unarmored and lacked self-sealing fuel tanks. In the Philippines this did not matter. It faced little fighter opposition and flew higher than antiaircraft fire could reach. (AC)

Philippine aircraft in the war's opening days, as they were the only aircraft capable of reaching deep into the Philippines from Formosa. They dominated the skies, and included:

**The Mitsubishi A6M (Zero, Zeke):** The infamous Mitsubishi *Reisen* (Zero) dominated the Pacific in 1941 and 1942, so much so that the Imperial Japanese Navy delayed developing a replacement. The Zeros used in the Philippines were the A6M2. They were armed with two 7.7mm machine guns and two Type 99-1 20mm cannon. It had a service ceiling of 32,000ft (9,750m) and a top speed of 332mph (530km/h). The A6M2 had a range of 2,575km (1,600 miles), allowing it to escort bombers from Formosa as far south as central Luzon. Some 107 A6Ms were stationed in Formosa at the start of the campaign.

**Mitsubishi G3M (Nell) and G4M (Betty):** These were two twin-engine bombers developed as long-range bombers for the Imperial Japanese Navy. These land-based attack bombers (*rikko*) were intended to offset Japanese naval treaty tonnage limitations by substituting aircraft for warships. They were effective ship killers early in the war, especially the G4M. Both carried one aerial torpedo or up to 800kg (1,766lb) of bombs. The G3M had a top speed of 233mph (375km/h), a cruising speed of 174mph (280km/h), and a range of 4,350km (2,700 miles). The G4M had a top speed of 365mph (590km/h), a cruising speed of 196mph (315km/h), and a range of 2,850km (1,770 miles). Badly protected with no armor and lacking self-sealing gasoline tanks, they were deadly when unopposed. There were 108 G3Ms and 48 G3Ms in Formosa.

## Facilities

Japan annexed Taiwan, which it named Formosa, from China in 1895 after winning the First Sino-Japanese War. It spent the next 46 years pacifying, industrializing, and militarizing its first colony. By 1941 it had an extensive system of naval ports, army bases, military airfields (both army and navy), and naval seaplane bases, throughout the island. It also had a robust transportation and industrial infrastructure capable of supporting these facilities.

The main airfields used by the 5th Hikoshidan units attacking the Philippines were at Heito, Chiatung, Choshu, Hengchun, and Pingtung Army Air Bases. The 5th Hikoshidan also had aircraft and base elements stationed in French Indochina, at Phnom Penh and Cam Rhan Bay. These played no part in the Philippine invasion.

Although the Imperial Army had airfields throughout Formosa, when the Pacific War started, all five airfields 5th Hikoshidan warplanes were operating out of were in the southern quarter of the island. (The 5th Hikoshidan had a transport *chutai* – squadron – at Taichung, in northern Formosa.) Hengchung is virtually at the southern tip of the island, around 175 miles from Luzon's north coast. The other four were 50–60 miles north of Hengchung.

Heito Airfield was the most important. It was home to the headquarters of the 5th Hikoshidan. Chiatung, in today's Taitung, headquartered the 4th Hikoden (Air Brigade) and Pingtung housed the headquarters of the 10th Hikoden. Pingtung and Hengchung were two of the oldest Imperial Army airfields in Formosa, dating to the 1920s. By the time the Pacific War started, Pingtung had paved runways, while Heito and Hengchung were primarily grass strips.

Bombers were stationed at Heito, Chiatung, Choshu, and Pingtung, with the heavier Ki-21s and Ki-48s at Chiatung and Choshu. Pingtung was used almost exclusively for light bombers, while Hengchung was a fighter strip. Hengchung also served as an emergency field, as it was closest to the Philippines. All major Imperial Army Formosa airfields had extensive maintenance and logistics facilities for their aircraft, even those with only grass runways.

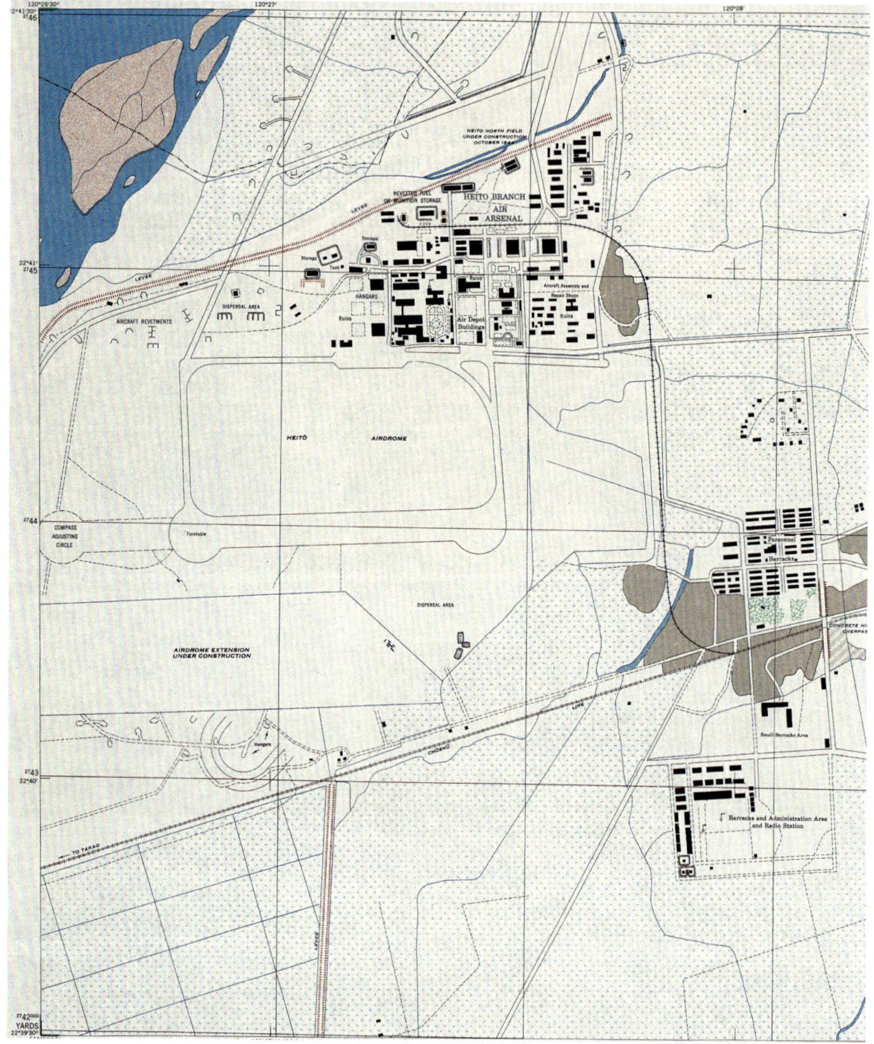


Japan had an extensive series of airfields in Formosa. This is a map of Heito, which contained an Imperial Army airfield and was built over what was once a horse racing track. An important Imperial Army fighter base, it was the location of the 5th Hikoshidan's headquarters. (AC)

The Imperial Navy's 11th Koku Kantai had two Koku Sentai (Naval Air Flotillas) in Formosa and one in Indochina. The Koku Sentai in Formosa were stationed at Takao, Tainan, and Taichung Naval Air Stations. There was also a seaplane base at Toko, from which a flying boat *kokutai* (squadron) operated.

Takao housed the Imperial Navy's oldest airfield in Formosa, entering service in 1933. It was collocated with the Imperial Navy's primary naval base in Formosa. The 21st Koku Sentai had its headquarters at Takao. Tainan was built in 1935 as a commercial airport, but was taken over by the Imperial Navy prior to the Pacific War. The 23rd Koku Sentai was headquartered there. Taichung was built in 1936 to support naval air operations against China. All three had paved runways and extensive fuel, supply, and maintenance facilities. All of these were large airfields, capable of supporting as many as 200 aircraft in a pinch.

These airfields were well-placed to support a Japanese invasion of the Philippines. Naval aircraft stationed in Formosa could easily hit targets as far south as Batangas on Luzon from their airfields. This included aircraft operating out of Taichung. The Ki-51 could easily reach Lingayen Bay (where the Japanese planned to invade) and go as far south as Clark Field with a reduced bombload. Only the Ki-27 was limited to the northern sliver of Luzon, and that only when operating from Hengchung.

The ability of the Imperial Army to operate its aircraft out of improvised and primitive airfields simplified its ability to provide direct air support to its ground forces. It facilitated the Japanese sieges of Bataan and Corregidor. (AC)

The Imperial Army's preference for grass fields was not due to aversion to paved runways or the economy gained by using grass or dirt landing strips; rather it was a means of practicing in the manner in which they intended to fight. The IJAAS was a tactical air force, intended to provide air support for Imperial Army ground forces. Experience in China showed its aircraft would often have to operate from unimproved airfields, especially its fighters and tactical bombers. It was one reason the Imperial Army retained fixed landing gear aircraft after other air forces moved to retractable gear. The simpler design was better suited to primitive conditions.

This led the IJAAS to design their ground support units for mobility. In addition to the standard aviation airbase ground support units fixed to a permanent airfield, the 5th Hikoshidan had mobile support units: two airbase ground support units, two labor and three airfield construction companies, two truck companies, two weather companies (with three weather station units), an air intelligence unit, and an antiaircraft battalion.

These forces accompanied the invasion forces headed to Aparri, Vigan, and Lingayen Bay. Once unloaded they could repair captured US airfields or create entirely new airfields from promising flat terrain. Once runways had been hacked out and cleared of obstructions, the airbase ground support unit could run the ground station, supported by trucked in fuel and ammunition. Weather and intelligence specialists could provide on the spot mission and operational planning. Moreover, the forward airfield would be protected by antiaircraft guns that kept pace with the support troops.

As the front moved, the forward air base could pack up everything and advance to a new position more convenient to providing the ground support the forward troops needed to continue an advance. It was a well-practiced exercise by 1941, honed by years of experience in China. It gave the IJAAS unprecedented mobility, something the US forces had not expected and could not counter. Within days of capturing an airfield, IJAAS were operating off it. The range limitations of short-ranged tactical aircraft were erased, and

Japan used mobile aviation ground support units throughout this campaign. This permitted rapid deployment of aircraft to forward bases. This is an Imperial Army weather unit operating out of a former US airfield captured in the Philippines. (AC)

the Imperial Army was able to push its control of the skies further over what had been enemy-controlled airspace.

## Weapons and tactics

Japan used a number of different weapons in this campaign, divided into three broad categories: aircraft guns, bombs intended for use against land and naval targets, and antiaircraft artillery, land-based, and aboard ships. The aircraft used in this campaign were armed with two principal types of guns: the 7.7mm machine gun and the 20mm cannon. As with everything else, the Imperial Army and Navy used different versions of the 7.7mm machine gun. (No Army aircraft in this campaign ordinarily carried 20mm cannon. When they did, they differed from the Navy 20mm.)

Four different versions of the 7.7mm machine guns were used, although three, the Imperial Army belt-fed Type 89 Model 2, the drum-fed Type 89, and Imperial Navy Type 97, were virtually identical. Additionally, the Imperial Navy used a Type 92 7.7mm machine gun. All were rifle-caliber guns, whose designs dated to World War I. The Type 89, Type 89 Model 2, and Type 97 machine guns were licensed copies of the British Vickers .303 machine guns. The Navy Type 92 was a licensed version of the British Lewis .303 machine gun.

The Type 89 Model 2 and Type 97 were belt-fed versions of the Vickers. On fighter aircraft, both the Ki-27 and the A6M, they were nose-mounted, synchronized to fire through the propeller arc. The Ki-30 and Ki-51 each carried one Type 89 machine gun wing-mounted, outside the propeller arc. The two types used different ammunition. The Type 89 was chambered for a slightly larger Japanese-developed cartridge, the 7.7x58mmSR, while the Type 97 used the standard British .303 cartridge. As a result, the ammunition of the two guns could not be interchanged.

The cartridge used for both Type 89 and Type 89 Model 2 yielded a higher muzzle velocity, but a lower rate of fire than the round used in the Type 97. The Type 89 had a rate of fire between 700 to 900 rounds per minute and a muzzle velocity of 820m/s (2,690ft/s) while the Type 97 could fire 1,000 rounds per minute with a muzzle velocity of 750m/s (2,460ft/s). Both had an effective range of 600m (1,970ft).

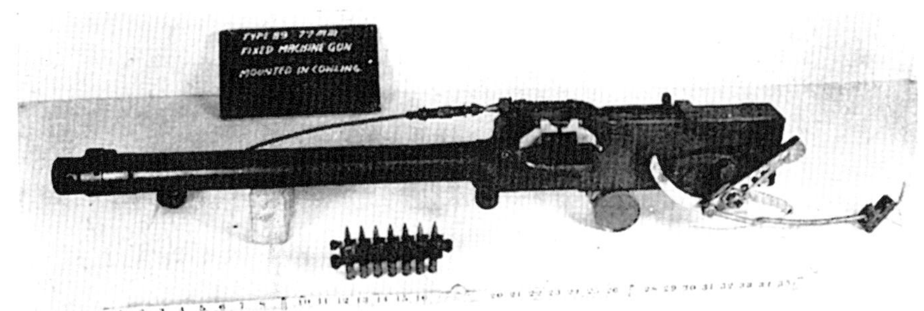


Four different versions of the 7.7mm machine gun served as the main weapon for Japanese aircraft in the Philippines. It was a rifle-caliber gun better suited for the 1930s than the 1940s. This is the Japanese Type 89 machine gun, used by Imperial Army aircraft. (AC)

The Type 89 had a drum magazine, and could be fitted with a flat drum magazine containing 69 rounds. It was used for hand-held flexible mountings on Imperial Army bombers. It had a rate of fire of 750 rounds per minute, a muzzle velocity of 747m/s (2,450ft/s) and an effective range of 600m (1,970ft).

The Type 92 was the Imperial Navy equivalent, used on the G4M and G3M bombers participating in this campaign. It could be fitted with a flat drum magazine carrying either 47 or 97 rounds. It could fire 600 rounds per minute, had a muzzle velocity of 762m/s (2,500ft/s), and an effective range of 600m (1,970ft). It was chambered for the same round as the Type 97.

All four 7.7mm machine guns were gas-actuated and air-cooled. The bullet massed 10–12g (depending on the type of round) with an energy of 3,300–3,500J (2,440–2,590ft lbf). This was satisfactory in the days when open-cockpit aircraft had wood framing and canvas covering, but by 1941 most US aircraft were metal clad and framed. A rifle-caliber round lacked the stopping power to easily bring down most multi-engine aircraft. While effective against troops in the open and unarmored aircraft, it was too light to reliably down the four-engine B-17.

The Japanese Navy recognized this deficiency and fitted the A6M with the Type 99 20mm machine gun. (The Japanese Navy called them machine guns rather than autocannon.) It was developed from Oerlikon 20mm. The version used in 1941 and throughout this campaign was the Type 99 Mark 1. They were air-cooled, gas-actuated, and belt-fed. It fired a 20x72RB cartridge with a projectile massing 200–203g, fired 520 rounds per minute, and had an effective range of 800m (2,625ft).

As with everything else, the Imperial Army and Navy employed different bombs, usable only by the service developing them. The most relevant to the Philippines were the Imperial Army high-explosive bomb series and the Imperial Navy's land and ordinary bombs. Both were high-explosive bombs, but the land bombs were intended for land targets, while the ordinary bombs were used against ships. Both services also had specialized bombs, not generally used in the Philippines.

Imperial Japanese Army bombers carried four types of bombs: The Type 94 50kg, the Type 94 or Type 1 100kg, and the Type 92 250kg and 500kg high-explosive bombs. All four had a cast-steel nosepiece connected to a tubular steel body, and a conical steel nosepiece to which four sheet steel fins were welded. All were filled with picric acid explosive, loaded in preformed paraffin-wrap blocks. The 50kg bomb was filled with 20kg (44lb) of explosive, the 100kg bomb with 47.75kg (103lb), the 250kg bomb with 104kg (230lb) and the 500kg bomb 223kg (491lb). The steel casing and fins made up the balance of the weight.

The Imperial Navy land and ordinary bombs were similar in function, but different in construction. The land bombs use less finished material. They consisted of three pieces, nose, cylindrical middle body, and tail cone, with the components welded or riveted together. Ordinary bombs had two-piece construction, with a unitary nose and body and the tail

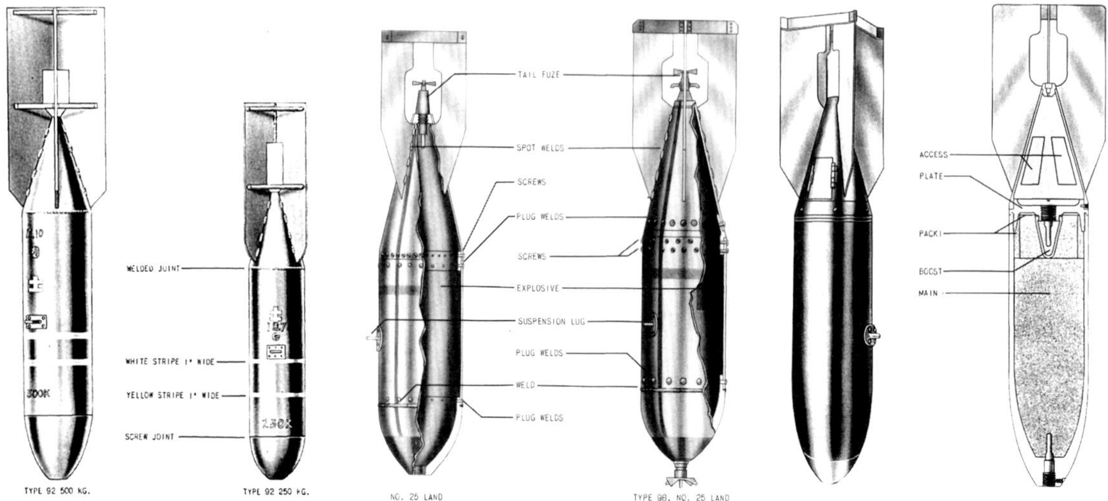


The Imperial Army typically used the Type 92 series high-explosive bombs in this campaign (left). The Navy used two different sets of bombs. Land bombs (center) were roughly built, screwed together and intended for use against stationary targets. Ordinary bombs (right) were more aerodynamic and intended for use against ships. (AC)

cone screwed into the rest of the bomb. They were machined inside and out and more aerodynamic than the land bombs.

The land bombs came in 55kg (124lb), 250kg (550lb), and 800kg (1,760lb) sizes. The standard bombs used were 60kg (132lb), 500kg (1,100lb), and 825kg (1,820lb) sizes. All used steel shells. The explosive used in all of these was picric acid, Type 98 explosive or TNT. Except for the 500kg ordinary bomb, the explosive made up 40–48 percent of the bomb's weight. The 500kg ordinary bomb was a penetrator, with only 67kg of Type 98 explosive. It was intended for use against armored warships.

The 50–60kg bomb was effective against troops in the open and aircraft on the ground, especially single-engine aircraft. The 100kg bomb could destroy a multi-engine aircraft, and potentially destroy or damage several. The larger bombs were more effective against buildings than parked aircraft due to their size. The blast radius was not significantly bigger than that of a 100kg bomb, and fewer could be carried. The 250kg bomb could take down the lightly constructed wood frame buildings typically used at allied airfields for maintenance shops, hangars, or warehouses. The 500kg and larger bombs could bring down a reinforced building. A direct hit by either would destroy a fuel or ammunition dump, even if stored in a bunker.

Japan brought the equivalent of four antiaircraft battalions to the Philippines. These units were equipped with three different weapons: the 7.7mm machine gun, the 20mm autocannon, and the Model 88 75mm antiaircraft gun. The 7.7mm antiaircraft gun was the Model 92. Its performance was virtually identical to the Type 89 machine gun used on Army aircraft. It had an effective range of 600m (1,970ft). The 20mm cannon was the Model 98. Introduced in 1938, it fired a 0.14kg round, had a 120 round per minute rate of fire, and an effective ceiling of 3,500ft (1,070m). The Model 88 75mm fired a 6.6kg (14.56lb) round. It could fire 15–20 rounds each minute with an effective ceiling of 21,000ft (6,400m). Antiaircraft played a very minor role due to early elimination of US air forces.

When the Pacific War started both IJA and IJN air forces were using tactics employed during the Second Sino-Japanese War. That is to say they were using the aerial tactics of the Great War. Even their organization reflected this. The *chutai* (or squadrons) were made up of three flights of three aircraft (with three reserve aircraft filling in when aircraft were out of service). They flew in tight vics of three aircraft. Each had an officer or senior NCO leading, a junior NCO in the second slot, and a trainee pilot in the third slot. In fighter units, the three aircraft operated together in a tight formation, until combat occurred.

In December 1941 Japan's air forces emphasized tight formation flying to and from a target, as demonstrated by this picture of Japanese bombers flying over Bataan. While in combat, formations would break up as fighters fought individual battles and individual bombers or bomber "vics" sought out targets on the ground. (AC)

Combat featured individual dogfights. Maneuverability was emphasized, almost exaggeratedly so. Pilots favored maneuverability over speed. Pilots disliked adding retractable landing gear because it added weight and reduced maneuverability. These tactics worked well against Chinese pilots of the Second Sino-Japanese war and well-enough in the initial phases of the Pacific War, when IJA pilots were engaging second-rate Allied aircraft in the opening months of the war, including in the Philippines.

Japanese air forces later used schwarm tactics employed initially by the Luftwaffe, and eventually by Allied air forces. The vic was replaced by the finger four, a loose formation made up of two pairs of two aircraft, with a lead and wingman in each pair, and one pair covering a lead pair. This deemphasized pure maneuverability, but better used the superior speed of retractable-gear closed-cockpit aircraft. However, these tactics were adopted after the active air phase of the Philippine campaign.

# DEFENDER'S CAPABILITIES

The B-17 was the USAAF's iconic strategic bomber in 1941. Its decision to commit one quarter of the then-operational B-17s to the Philippines indicated the USAAF's belief in the capability of the bomber to deter aggression and its faith in the Flying Fortress as an effective weapon of war. (NMAF)

Defending the Philippines from air attack and invasion was the US Army Air Force's Far East Air Force (FEAF), the United States Navy, and the antiaircraft elements in the ground forces of the US Army. These were attached to the Coastal Artillery Command, guarding Philippine coastal forts or a mobile antiaircraft regiment at Fort Stotsenburg, collocated with Clark Field. (A second antiaircraft regiment was organized after the war began.) No US Army units or Philippine Army units had organizational antiaircraft.

The FEAF consisted of the 5th Bomber and 5th Fighter Commands (which would be reorganized into the V Air Force after leaving the Philippines), the Philippine Army Air Corps (PAAC), and the base element at the US and Philippine Army airfields in

The P-40 was the most advanced fighter the United States had in the Philippines. It was superior to every Japanese aircraft used in the invasion, except the A6M Zero. Unfortunately, the Zero was its primary opponent during the campaign. (AC)

the Philippine Commonwealth. There was also a small US Navy aviation component, primarily two patrol wings of Consolidated PBY Catalina and antiaircraft assets guarding the US Naval Base at Cavite.

Although the FEAF had numerous aircraft and widespread facilities, the majority of the aircraft were obsolescent, the facilities suffered from neglect, and the logistics infrastructure was inadequate to support sustained aerial combat. The Army attempted to reverse these trends at the beginning of 1941. A combination of distance and lack of available resources meant few of the reinforcements arrived and few of the improvements had been completed before war overtook the Philippines. It was an excellent illustration of fighting a war with the resources at hand rather than the resources planned for the campaign.

## Aircraft

The US FEAF had over 300 aircraft. Of these, 50-odd were trainers. Of the warplanes, perhaps 150 were operational. These included 54 P-40E and 18 P-40B fighters, approximately 20 P-35A and 12 P-26A fighters, up to 10 B-12, and up to 18 B-18 bombers, 33 to 35 B-17C and B-17D heavy bombers, and 9 A-27 attack aircraft. The P-26s and B-10s were part of the PAAC. The rest of the warplanes belonged to the US Army Air Forces. There was also a US Navy contingent of 36 PBY-3 and PBY-4 amphibians. These aircraft had the following characteristics:

**Curtis P-40B Tomahawk and P40E Warhawk:** These were the most modern fighters in the FEAF. It could hold its own against the A6M, and was clearly superior to the Ki-27. A development of the radial-engine Curtis P-36 Hawk, replacing the radial engine with a more powerful inline engine, it was the most advanced operational fighter in the USAAF inventory when World War II began. They were single-engine, all-metal aircraft with enclosed cockpits, and retractable landing gear.

The P-40B had an Allison V-1710-33 engine generating 1040hp. It had a top speed of 352mph (566km/h), cruised at 225mph (362km/h), had a 32,400ft (9,900m) ceiling and 1,175km (730 miles) range. The P-40E, with an improved version of the V-1710 generating 1150hp maxed its speed at 362mph (583km/h) and cruised at 235mph (380km/h) with a 30,000ft (9,150m) ceiling and a range of 1,370km (850 miles). The P-40B had two cowl-mounted Browning M-2 .50cal machine guns and four wing-mounted Browning M1919 .30cal machine guns; the P-40E had six wing-mounted M-2 Browning .50cal machine guns.

**Seversky P-35:** The P-35 (which never acquired a nickname) was the first all-metal, enclosed-cockpit retractable-gear fighter aircraft in the Army Air Corps inventory, first seeing service in 1937. It was quickly superseded by the P-36 and P-40. Seversky kept it in production for export. Half of these exports were embargoed, and accepted into the USAAF as the P-35A in June 1940. Some were sent to the Philippines in February 1941 for transfer to the PAAC, although most were still operated by the USAAF when the war began.

The P-35A was powered by a single Pratt & Whitney R-1830-45 Twin Wasp radial engine, generating 1,050hp (780kW). It had a top speed of 290mph (467km/h), cruised at 260mph (418km/h), had a service ceiling of 31,400 ft (9,600m), and a 1,530km (950 miles) range. It was armed with two cowl-mounted Browning M-2 .50cal machine guns and two wing-mounted Browning M1919 .30cal machine guns. It carried up to 160kg (350lb) of bombs.

**Boeing P-26A (Peashooter):** The Peashooter was the US Army Air Corps' (USAAC) hottest fighter in 1932. Ten years later it was obsolete. A low-wing, open cockpit, fixed-gear monoplane with wire-braced wings, it had been largely retired from the US inventory by 1940. However, 26 had been sent to the Philippines for use by the PAAC. Even there it was due to be phased out in 1942.

It was powered by one Pratt & Whitney R-1340-27 Wasp 9-cylinder air-cooled radial engine, generating 600hp (450kW). It had a top speed of 234mph (377km/h), a 27,400ft

(8,400m) service ceiling, and a 580km (360 miles) combat range. It was armed with 2 × .30in (7.62mm) M1919 Browning machine guns and could carry two 55kg (100lb) bombs.

**Boeing B-17 (Flying Fortress):** The B-17 was the first mass-produced four-engine bomber to enter service in the US armed forces. It was a long-range, low-wing, all-metal aircraft with retractable landing gear and enclosed cockpit. The US sent most of its available B-17s to the Philippines in 1941. Its role was to intercept invasion fleets before they reached the beaches and sink them at sea. Fortresses sent to the Philippines were early-model B-17Cs and B-17Ds. Only a combined total of 80 B-17Cs and B-17Ds were built.

These versions were powered by four turbocharged Wright R-1820-65 9-cylinder, air-cooled single-row radial engines delivering 1,200hp (850kW). The B-17C had a top speed of 308mph (496km/h), cruised at 227mph (365km/h), had a 5,500km (3,400 miles) range, and a 36,000ft (10,973m) ceiling. The B-29D had a top speed of 318mph (512km/h), cruised at 226mph (364km/h), had a 3,950km (2,450 miles) range, and a 37,800ft (11,520m) ceiling. Both were armed with six flexible Browning M2 .50cal machine guns and a single, flexible Browning M1919 .30cal machine gun in the nose. Maximum bomb load was 1,800kg (4,000lb). B-17s had a crew of eight: pilot, co-pilot, navigator, bombardier, flight engineer, radio operator, and two gunners.

**Douglas B-18 (Bolo):** The aircraft that won the 1935 bomber competition in which the B-17 debuted, it was inferior to the B-17 and most other medium bombers of its generation. The best that can be said of it was that it was clearly superior to the B-10 it replaced. A bomber version of the DC-2 airliner, it was weakly armed, poorly protected, with indifferent performance. By 1940 it was the standard USAAC bomber. By 1941 it was being phased out. Thereafter it was used exclusively as an antisubmarine warfare aircraft.

The B-18s in the Philippines were powered by two Wright R-1820-53 Cyclone 9-cylinder air-cooled radial engines producing 1,000hp (750kW), giving it a maximum speed of 217mph (349km/h), cruising speed of 167mph (269km/h), a 23,900ft (7,300m) ceiling, and combat range of 1,370km (850 miles). It had a crew of six and was armed with three hand-held, flexibly mounted Browning M1919 .30cal machine guns. Its standard bombload was 910kg (2,000lb).

**Martin B-10:** When it entered service in 1934, the B-10 was ahead of its time, the first bomber to simultaneously incorporate all-metal construction, retractable landing gear, enclosed cockpits, and rotating gun turrets. By 1941 it was obsolete, and the US consigned theirs in the Philippines to the PAAC (presumably for bomber training, although B-10s attempted to fly combat missions in December 1941).

It was powered by two Wright R-1820-33 Cyclone (F-3) 9-cylinder air-cooled radial engines generating 775hp (578kW), permitting a top speed of 213mph (343km/h) and cruising speed of 193mph (311km/h). Its service ceiling was 24,200ft (7,400m) and it had a 2,000km (1,240 miles) range. It had a crew of four, and was armed with three Browning M1919 .30cal machine guns, and carried a 1,025kg (2,260lb) maximum bombload.

**The North American Aviation A-27:** An attack version of the T-6 Texan advanced trainer. Ten were ordered by Siam (Thailand) in 1939, but the order was taken over by the USAAC in October 1940 to prevent them from being used

The A-27 were aircraft confiscated from a shipment going to the Kingdom of Siam. They were sent to the Philippines because the USAAF had no need for them, and thought they could fill a combined role as a close-support aircraft and an advanced trainer for the PAAC. All six sent were destroyed when Japan attacked Nichols Field. (NMAF)

by Japan (Siam was allied with Japan). The aircraft, designated A-27, were sent to the Philippines, where they were used as advanced trainers and attack aircraft.

It was powered by a 785hp (585kW) air-cooled Wright R-1820 radial engine. It had a top speed of 250mph (402km/h), an 1,290km (800 miles) range, and a service ceiling of 28,000ft (8,530m). It had a crew of two (pilot and gunner) and was armed with three Browing M1919 .30cal machine guns, two fixed forward-firing, and one aft flexible mount. It caried four 55kg (100lb) bombs on underwing racks.

**Consolidated PBY (Catalina):** This was a twin-engine, parasol-wing flying boat used as both a long-range scout, search-and-rescue craft and bomber. All PBYs in the Philippines were purely flying boats, lacking landing gear. PBY-3s and PBY-4s lacked the blister waist .50cal positions of PBY-5s and later. They had flat panels. The Catalina was slow and ungainly, but used properly they were highly effective and even deadly.

The PBY-3 had two Pratt & Whitney Twin Wasp 1,000hp (750kW) R-1830-66 engines. Its maximum speed was 191mph (307km/h). It had a 24,100ft (7,345m) service ceiling and a patrol range of 3,430km (2,131 miles). The PBY-4 with 1,050hp R-1830-72 Twin Wasps had the same service ceiling, but a top speed of 198mph (319km/h) and a patrol range of 3,500km (2,175 miles). Both were armed with two Browning M1919 .30cal machine guns (one in a bow turret and one in a ventral hatch in the tail) and two M2 .50cal machine guns, one each in waist hatches. It carried up to 1,814kg (4,000lb) of bombs.

## Facilities

The United States occupied the Philippines in 1898. It developed an extensive network of naval and army facilities to maintain control of the islands. Most of the highly developed ones, including massive fortifications built to guard Manila Bay and the Philippines's major port, Manila, were built prior to World War I and located on Luzon, the Philippines's largest and most important island.

As a result of the 1922 Washington Naval Limitations Treaty, no further development of fortifications was permitted until after Japan withdrew from the Washington Treaty in 1936.

Iba Field, center left, was typical of the airfields the US built in the Philippines. It had an unpaved runway, with a few basic buildings to shelter and service the aircraft stationed there. One of two active radar stations in the Philippines was located at Iba Field. (NARA)

Since the US was then at the nadir of the Great Depression, no further work on fortifications was done until World War II started in 1939.

The treaty did not forbid the construction of airfields, only their fortification. As aviation grew in importance in the 1920s and 1930s, the US Army and the US Colonial Authority authorized and constructed airfields throughout the Philippines, both military and civilian. The US Navy limited its aviation activities in the Philippines to three seaplane bases.

Most airfields were simple grass or gravel airstrips, like most airfields throughout the world during the 1920s and 1930s. Dozens appeared as air travel was frequently the fastest way to move around the Philippines's many islands that were jungle-covered with scant road systems. Typically, a runway was cleared and few simple support structures were thrown up: hangars, barracks, fueling facilities, and, for civilian fields, passenger depots. As with many small airfields in the US, they were low-tech, wood frame buildings with basic service facilities. Much of the maintenance fell under the category of shade-tree mechanics, rudimentary structures with hand-operated equipment.

By their nature, even simple civilian airfields were dual purpose. Fighter aircraft of the day and most bombers could operate from them, even if ordinance had to be moved in. The Army Air Corps also had three long-standing improved airfields in the Philippines: Clark, Nichols, and Nielson Field in Luzon. It was also building a major bomber field in Mindanao, at a former Del Monte plantation.

Clark and Nichols Fields were established in 1919; Nielson Field was built in 1937 as a civilian airport and taken over by the US military in 1940 or 1941. Del Monte was a war-emergency effort started in 1941. All three of the Luzon airfields had paved runways, extensive metal-framed or masonry buildings, and full aviation maintenance facilities. Clark and Nichols were where most FEAF aircraft were permanently stationed. Nielson served as FEAF and PAAC headquarters, and served as the primary flight school. The remaining USAAF airfields were auxiliary fields which served to disperse aircraft.

Work on Del Monte started in November 1941. When the Pacific War started it had three long grass runways, fueling facilities, and not much else. Personnel were housed in tents and only rudimentary logistical and maintenance facilities existed. Similar to the major Luzon airfields, Del Monte had three auxiliary airfields to which aircraft could be dispersed.

The PAAC used Nielson Field as its maintenance center, logistical hub, and flying school. In addition, it maintained around a dozen outlying airfields. Although many were in Luzon, others were scattered throughout the Philippines, in Cebu, Leyte, and Mindanao. They were equivalent to the USAAF auxiliary airfields in terms of runways and facilities.

The US Navy's aerial contribution was maritime. It had three fixed seaplane bases (at Cavite and Olongapo in Luzon, and Malalag Bay in Midanao) and four seaplane tenders: USS *Langley*, *Childs*, *W. B. Preston*, and *Heron*. All four were conversions. *Langley* was formerly an aircraft carrier, *Childs* and *W. B. Preston* former destroyers, and *Heron* a minesweeper.

While there were appropriate base support elements at the major airfields, there were not enough resources to support a protracted campaign. Worse, support elements were tied to their airfields, in hard to relocate permanent structures. This was a garrison air force. If the major airfields were lost, so too, was the capability to service, repair, and arm aircraft. Complicating things further, the airfields had no defense against air attack other than their fighter detachments. There was almost no antiaircraft artillery (except for four antiaircraft battalions), few revetments or sheltered parking for aircraft, and the buildings were not reinforced or fortified.

Nor were any naval or army installations fortified against air attack. Even the fortifications guarding Manila Bay were designed only to withstand naval bombardment. They had been designed and built prior to the aircraft being a threat. The ability to survive a 14in shell hit gave some protection against air attack, but the 12in mortars at these forts were

Cavite was located on a peninsula on the southern shore of Manila Bay. It was the US Navy's biggest facility in Asia. Since it was within the perimeter guarded by the Manila Bay forts it was secure from naval attack, but lay exposed to air attack, rendering it useless to the US Navy. (USNHHC)

in sunken, open-topped positions. These were virtually invulnerable to naval gunfire, but naked to air attack.

The US also stopped improving its military installations, army, navy, and air force, in the Philippines in 1935, once the Commonwealth was on the path to independence. This was reversed only in 1940 as tensions with Japan grew. Any real buildup started in early 1941, when the US began pouring available resources into the Philippines. Unfortunately, there were relatively few available resources to send. Well over half the available B-17s were sent to the Philippines with 36 actually on the islands when the war started. (Another batch of Philippine-bound B-17Cs and Ds arrived at Oahu just as the Japanese fleet launched its aerial assault on Pearl Harbor.) Additional fighters, antiaircraft artillery, and support units were being sent when the war started.

The permanent US airfields in the Philippines had extensive maintenance facilities, such as this engine shop at Nichols Field. They were necessary, but could not be moved. This made the US Army reluctant to abandon these airfields. (NARA)

However, there was a shortage of spare parts for USAAF aircraft in 1941. To increase aircraft production, spares procurement had been slashed, to be made up the following year. The Philippines were at the end of a long supply chain, at the periphery of US interests, which were focused on Europe. Spares sent were siphoned off by quartermasters closer to the source of supply to make up their own shortages. The stores of ammunition and fuel, especially live bombs, .50cal ammunition, and 100 octane gasoline, were well below levels needed for military action.

The result was that the FEAF was short of everything but .30cal bullets and practice bombs. Its infrastructure and logistics were adequate for peacetime operations, but could not support a major war. Worse, a sense of complacency pervaded upper command. While aware of the shortcomings of their own air forces, all but a handful (such as Asiatic Fleet commander Thomas Hart) were convinced the Japanese were less prepared than the US–Filipino forces.

## Weapons and tactics

The weapons used by FEAF and US Navy aircraft in the Philippines included the Browning M2 .50cal and M1919 .30cal machine guns, and a variety of bombs. On the ground it had antiaircraft artillery (mostly 3in antiaircraft guns and .30cal and .50cal machine guns) and a rudimentary air warning system, including two radar sets.

The M2 .50cal was a highly reliable, air-cooled machine gun. Navy, Army, and Filipino aircraft used a dedicated aircraft version, the AN/M2 (where AN stood for Army–Navy). The M2 had a muzzle velocity of 2,910fps. It fired 750 to 850 rounds per minute. The gun fired a 52g bullet, capable of penetrating 1in of armor and the structural steel of unarmored ships. The Army and Navy also had standard versions used with ground forces and ships as antiaircraft guns. Their performance was similar.

The M1919 was lighter, firing an 11g round with a muzzle velocity of 2,800fps. It was an air-cooled development of the Browning M1917 water-cooled .30cal machine gun (some of which were in service in the Philippine Army and the US Navy, including as antiaircraft guns). Aircraft versions fired 1,200–1,500 rounds per minute. It was effective primarily against aircraft or troops in the open. It had an effective range of 1,500yds. As an antiaircraft weapon it was ineffective against aircraft over 500ft above it.

The US armed forces in the Philippines used a variety of prewar aerial bombs. These were not the "AN" bombs used by both US Army Air Forces and US Navy aircraft later in the war. The Amy used the "Modified Mark" series, the "M" series, and the Navy used the "Mk" series bombs in the Philippines.

The "Modified Mark" bombs had streamlined bodies for the 100lb, 300lb, and 600lb versions used in the Philippines, and cylindrical bodies with an aerodynamic nose cone and conical tail cone for the 2,000lb version. (The 1,100lb and 2,000lb versions do not appear to have been used in the Philippines.) They were made from three cast-steel sections welded together, and were filled with cast TNT. They were filled with 65lb, 148lb, and 355lb of explosive respectively.

The "M" series had cylindrical bodies with an ovoid nose and a truncated cylinder tail. They were manufactured from seamless steel tubing with a swaged nose, and sheet steel tailfins. They were filled with either 50–50 Amatol and TNT, or 100 percent TNT. They came in 100lb (M30), 300lb (M31), and 600lb (M33) sizes. They were termed "Demolition" bombs.

The 100lb size of both types was the most commonly used in the Philippines by the Army Air Force and PAAC. Bomb-armed fighters

US air forces in the Philippines lacked the hemispherical-nose, cylindrical-bodied "AN" bombs used through the rest of the war. They used prewar inventories of bombs. These included the Army demolition bombs shown here. The 600lb bomb was used by Colin Kelly when he attacked *Natori*. (AC)

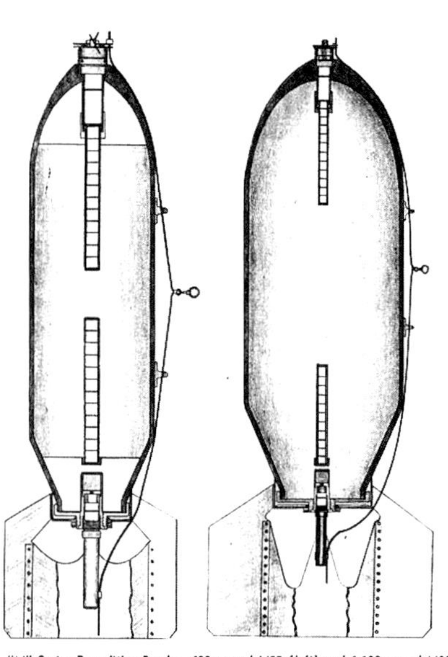
"M" Series Demolition Bombs—600-pound M32 (left) and 1,100-pound M33 (right)

carried 100lb bombs almost exclusively. The 300lb bombs and 600lb bombs were carried by bombers. B-10s and B-18s were to be armed with 100lb and 300lb bombs, depending on the mission. B-17s carried a mix of bombs, including the 600lb bombs.

The prewar US Navy used bombs different yet similar to those used by the US Army. Present in the Philippines were the 100lb GP (general purpose) Mark 1 and Mark 4 bombs, and 500lb GP Marks 3, 9, and 12. The 100lb bombs had a sheet steel cast body, while the 500lb bomb was one-piece forged steel. These bombs were filled with TNT: the Mark 1 had 65lb, the Mark 4 55lb, and the various 500lb bombs 256lb. Catalinas carried 500lb bombs or a mix of 100lb and 500lb bombs.

The 100lb bomb was effective against troops in the open, aircraft on the ground, and motor vehicles, but did relatively little damage to ships and standard buildings. The 300lb bomb was effective against buildings, railroad locomotives, and would create significant damage to a ship. A single 600lb bomb would sink a standard cargo ship or small warship (below the size of destroyers), while multiple hits would sink or cripple all but the most heavily armored naval vessels.

The largest antiaircraft guns fielded by either service were 3in antiaircraft guns. Even these were scarce.

The US Army in the Philippines was largely equipped with the 3in/40cal M1903 and its variants (M1903, M1917, and M1918) and the 1938 3in M3. The M1903 was originally introduced in 1903 as a coastal gun, and was modified into an antiaircraft gun in 1917 with a high-angle mount and further improved in 1918. The high-angle mount was added to some of the M1903s in the Philippines. These guns fired a 15lb round with a normal rate of fire of 12 rounds per minute. Its ceiling was 26,000ft, but it was rarely effective above 18,000ft.

They were present at Coastal Defense fortifications around Manila Bay, typically two to four guns at each, although Corregidor had 28 scattered among five batteries on the island. There were also two antiaircraft regiments, the 60th Coastal Artillery (AA) at Fort Mills in Manila Bay and the 200th at Fort Stotsenburg near Angeles City, Luzon. Each had 12 3in guns, although only the guns at Fort Stotsenburg were mobile.

The US Navy used two different 3in antiaircraft guns in the Philippines, the indifferent 3in/23cal, and the excellent, albeit light 3in/50cal. The 3in/23cal was originally a boat and landing gun upgraded into an antiaircraft gun in World War I. It fired a 16.5lb round with a .74lb bursting charge. It could fire nine rounds per minute and had a ceiling of 18,000ft, although it was ineffective above 12,000ft.

With a gun design dating to pre-World War I and a mounting developed during the Great War, the 3in/.40cal M1918 was the heaviest antiaircraft gun available to US forces in the Philippines. It lacked the ceiling to reach the altitudes at which Japanese level bombers operated, and was further handicapped by faulty ammunition (AC)

The 3in/50cal became operational in 1915, and was much more effective. It fired a 24lb round with a .74lb bursting charge. It could fire 15 rounds per minute, and with a well-trained crew up to 20 rounds. It had a 29,000ft ceiling, although it was generally ineffective above 24,000ft.

As with the Army, the Navy had relatively few 3in antiaircraft guns. Cavite had a nine-gun battery protecting it. The Naval Inshore Patrol squadron, the only forces in the Philippines when the war started, also had gunboats armed with 3in antiaircraft guns, either as secondary or main batteries.

Other than 3in antiaircraft guns, the only antiaircraft weapons available were the Navy 1.1in/75 quad gun, 37mm cannon, and .50cal and .30cal machine guns, a mix of Browning M2, M1917, and M1918 guns, described earlier, but on ground mounts. These had a ceiling of 4,000ft and were rarely effective above 2,000ft. As with the antiaircraft artillery, there were too few to provide an effective air defense, and were only useful against very low-flying aircraft. In addition to the machine guns at the coastal forts, each antiaircraft regiment had 12 machine guns and 24 37mm antiaircraft guns.

Among the reinforcements sent to the Philippines before the war began were seven SCR-270 mobile radar sets. They could be transported in six vehicles, and required a crew of 50 to operate around the clock. They broadcast in VHF, from 104 to 112MHz, and detected aircraft as far away as 250 miles, although 150 miles was more typical. Accurate to four miles and two degrees, they provided range and bearing. Even at 150 miles they provided 30–45 minutes advanced warning.

They should have been a game-changer, but their usefulness was handicapped by primitive radar doctrine and limited personnel trained as operators. Only two of the seven sets were operational on December 8, one at Ewa Field and one north of Manila. The radar information was not distributed in a timely fashion, either.

The radars reported observations to Nichols Field, which collected it and then sent alerts to the appropriate airfields and potential targets. The destination facilities then distributed the information as they saw applicable. All communication was sent by secure teletype, which had to be deciphered. The process took time, as much as an hour from detection of incoming enemy aircraft until warnings reached interested parties. By then the raid was either already in progress or over.

Like the Japanese, US and Filipino air forces used tactics dating to World War I. Both fighters and bombers used tight three-aircraft "vic" formations, with the junior pilots conforming to the movements of the formation's senior, up to the initiation of combat, for fighter pilots. Once in combat, maneuvering was stressful, despite the US superiority in firepower and generally speed. Dogfighting played to the Japanese strengths, while reducing the opportunities to use US aircraft advantages. Hit-and-run tactics were then being developed by the Flying Tigers in China, and adoption of loose "finger-four" schwarm tactics pioneered by the Luftwaffe, even innovations such as the "Thatch Weave" lay in the future. Inadequate US tactics contributed to US aerial failure in the Philippines.

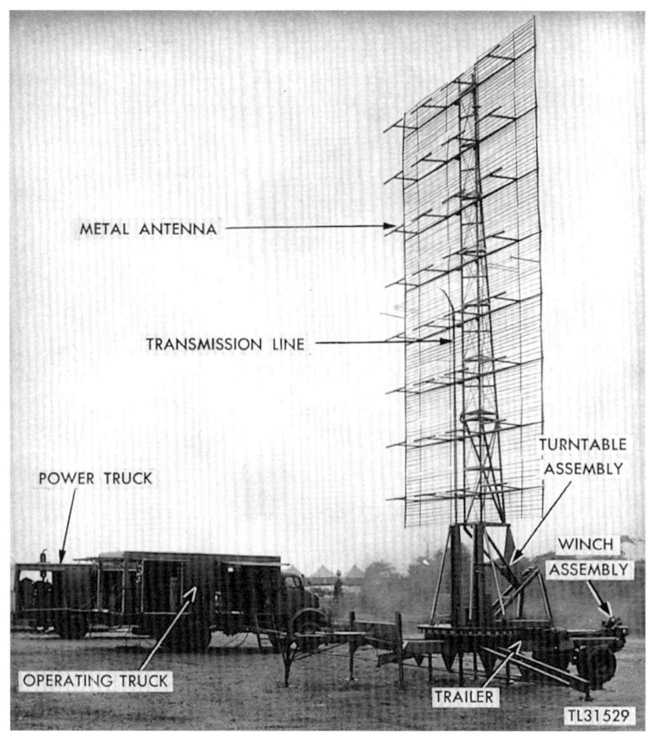


The US Army sent seven SCR-270 radar sets. They were portable, and the unit required six trucks to move the whole unit. Due to crew shortages, only two SCR-270s were operational when the war began and one was destroyed on the war's opening day. (AC)

# CAMPAIGN OBJECTIVES

Lacking other forces available, the Army Air Forces decided to send B-17s to the Philippines. They were then the most powerful aircraft in the US inventory. They could be moved to the Philippines quickly, since their range allowed them to fly to the Philippines by island-hopping from California across the Pacific. (NMAF)

The battle for the Philippines in 1941–42 was a result of Japanese actions in China, and US reaction to those events. Japan had been carving off pieces of China since 1895, when it annexed Formosa (today's Taiwan); it annexed the Liaotung Peninsula in the wake of the 1904–05 Russo-Japanese War; and controlled Korea, which had been a Chinese client state until 1895, from 1906 on, formally annexing it in 1910. Distracted by World War I, Japan returned in 1931 to seize control of Manchuria, which it renamed Manchukuo.

Having succeeded previously, Japan made another land grab in China in 1937, seizing the northeastern Chinese provinces closest to Manchukuo. They quickly captured China's most important port, Shanghai, and China's then-capital city, Nanking. Yet despite worldwide condemnation, no other nation, including the US, intervened, militarily or economically.

It looked as if Japan's gamble had paid off. However, China refused to surrender, even when Japan captured China's new capital city, Wuhan. China's Kuomintang Nationalist government, led by Chiang Kai Shek, simply moved its capital deep within China, out of Japan's reach, and continued fighting. The government knew it could not throw the Japanese out. Equally, they knew Japan lacked the manpower to physically occupy all of China. If China stayed in the war, Japan could not consolidate its latest conquest. The Kuomintang hoped it could wait Japan out. Alternatively, something else might happen to distract Japan.

Japan, unwilling to withdraw, and determined to win the war, decided to besiege China, isolating China from the world. Without food and military supplies, Free China's people would starve and its army would collapse. In 1938 Japan began occupying Chinese ports. By 1939 Japan occupied or controlled access to every major port on China's coast. The US, Britain, and France complained, but again did not intervene.

China was receiving supplies through the French colony of Indochina. When France fell to Germany, Japan saw a way to close that route. In the summer of 1940, using military action and diplomacy, Japan forced France to permit the Japanese occupation of Tonkin, Indochina's northern province.

At that point, the US had enough. Widening the war outside China threatened all European and American colonies in Asia. It wanted Japan contained. The US embargoed scrap iron

**OPPOSITE** STRATEGIC OVERVIEW

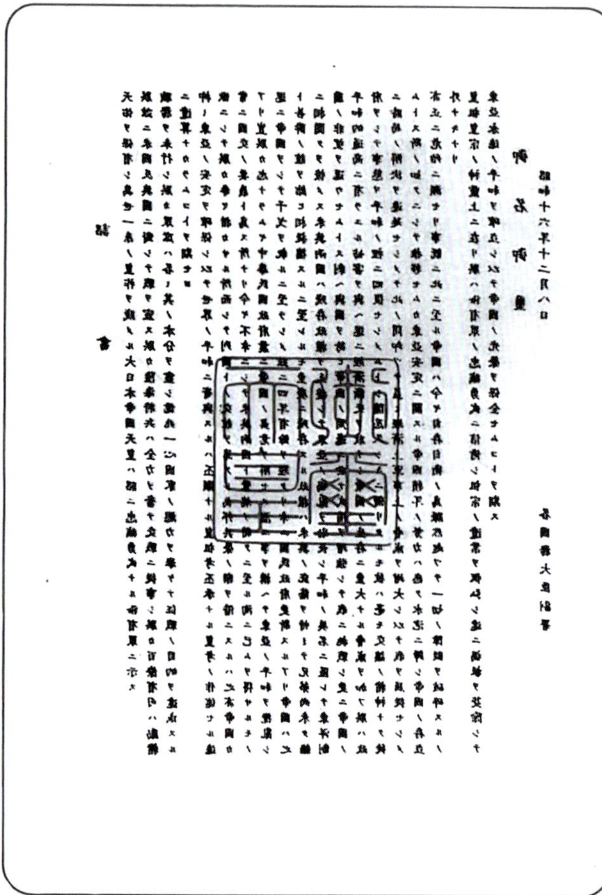

A copy of the Imperial Rescript containing the declaration of war by Japan against the United States. It cites the economic embargo imposed by the United States and the reinforcement of military forces in the Far East as the main causes for the declaration. (AC)

and steel to Japan. It began providing China with military aid and reinforcing the Philippines.

Instead of restraining Japan, this inflamed them. Intent on strangling China, Japan moved into the rest of Indochina in July 1941. The US, Britain, and the Netherlands all reacted. The US froze all Japanese assets in the United States, and Britain and the Netherlands joined the US in an embargo of petroleum products to Japan. At that time Japan imported 88 percent of its petroleum, 80 percent from the US; the US and its allies believed this would force Japan to disgorge Indochina.

Japan had under a year before its oil ran out, and its economy and military ground to a halt. Rather than back down, it decided to seize the oil it needed, moving into the British and Dutch oilfields surrounding the South China Sea. It would use its new bases in Indochina as a springboard to seize Malaya and the Dutch East Indies. However, the Philippines were in the way. Japan decided to take them, too.

## Japanese objectives

Japan did not really want the Philippines. What Japan wanted was the petroleum, rubber, and tin in the Dutch East Indies and British holdings around the South China Sea. The Philippines were between Japan and what they really wanted. Japan felt it could not afford to bypass the Philippines and simply take the British and Dutch colonies, even if the US remained neutral. In US hands the Philippines threatened Japanese communications with the South China Sea's periphery.

Although Japan did not want the Philippines, it needed control of them to further its strategic goals. Its long-term plan went beyond the Dutch East Indies and the British colonies in the Far East. It needed to hold them. Prewar planning intended to establish a defensive perimeter beyond them. Japan planned to seize territory in an arc running from Burma, along the southern islands of the Dutch East Indies, New Guinea north of the Owen Stanley Range, New Britain and New Ireland, and through the coral atolls of the Central Pacific, and from there to the Aleutians. Once this perimeter was secured, it would be fortified.

Japan's leaders believed any threat to their hegemony must come from their east or southeast. Britain was fully engaged in Europe, the Netherlands were occupied by Germany, and Australia was sparsely populated, with little industrial capacity. None of them had enough strategic capital to launch an offensive from the west or south; only the US could seriously challenge Japan. East, or possibly southeast, were the directions from which the US was bound to come. It was the shortest route from the US to Japan.

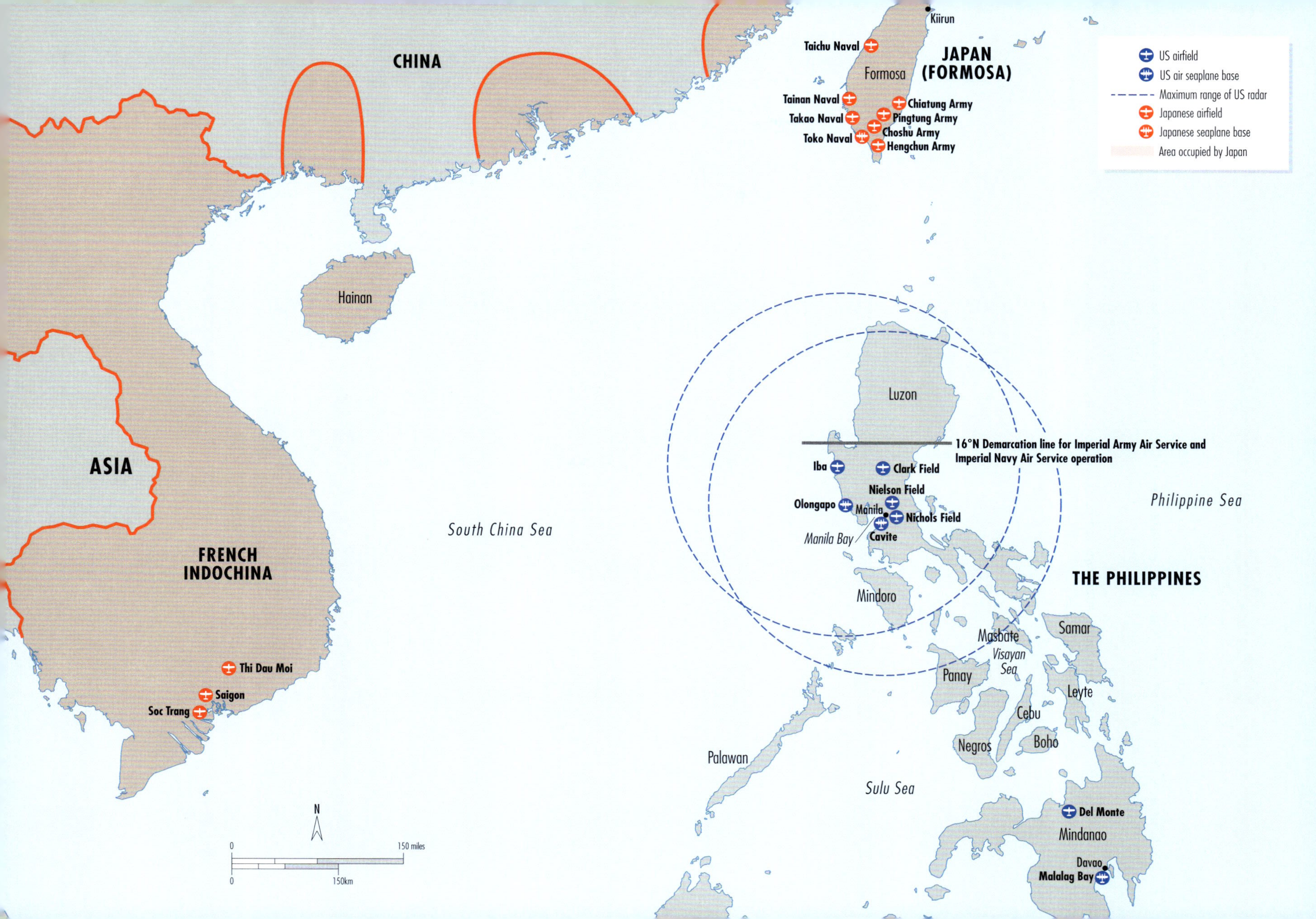

CHINA
JAPAN (FORMOSA)
Formosa
Kiirun
Taichu Naval
Tainan Naval
Takao Naval
Toko Naval
Chiatung Army
Pingtung Army
Choshu Army
Hengchun Army
US airfield
US air seaplane base
Maximum range of US radar
Japanese airfield
Japanese seaplane base
Area occupied by Japan
Hainan
ASIA
FRENCH INDOCHINA
Thi Dau Moi
Saigon
Soc Trang
South China Sea
Luzon
16°N Demarcation line for Imperial Army Air Service and Imperial Navy Air Service operation
Iba
Clark Field
Nielson Field
Olongapo
Manila
Nichols Field
Manila Bay
Cavite
Philippine Sea
THE PHILIPPINES
Mindoro
Masbate
Visayan Sea
Samar
Panay
Leyte
Cebu
Negros
Boho
Palawan
Sulu Sea
Del Monte
Mindanao
Davao
Malalag Bay
N
0
150 miles
0
150km

Japan did not want the Philippines. What they wanted was control of the oilfields and refineries, such as this one in Balikpapan, Borneo. The Philippines lay between Japan and the petroleum Japan desired. As a result, Japan needed to take it whether they wanted it or not. (USNHHC)

Japan intended to force the US to batter its way across the Pacific or South Pacific through several rings of fortified islands. Japan believed at some point the US would become exhausted, and settle for a negotiated peace, allowing Japan to retain its South China Sea gains. But just as the Philippines controlled communications between Japan and the South China Sea, it also stood astride the routes to the southeastern ring of Japan's intended defensive perimeter. In enemy hands, it cut the lines to those outposts. The Philippines had to be taken, and it had to be taken quickly.

The upcoming Japanese offensive was scheduled to be completed, to the planned outer defensive perimeter, within six months. New Britain and New Ireland were on the far side of the Philippines. It had to be taken economically. When December 1941 started, Japan had 52 active divisions, most tied down in China or homeland defense. Only ten were available for Japan's Southern Expeditionary Army, and only two infantry divisions and an infantry brigade were allocated to taking the Philippines. Similarly, while the Imperial Army's Air Force had the equivalent of six Hikoshidan, only two were available for the offensive and the more powerful of those was committed to Southeast Asia. Only one was committed to the Philippines.

Nor was the Imperial Navy's contribution generous. Most of the Imperial Navy was committed elsewhere, including the Pearl Harbor force, on operations in the Pacific, and supporting activities against the Dutch East Indies and the Malay Peninsula. A light carrier with its destroyer escort was committed to support invasions on Southern Luzon and Mindanao. Five destroyer divisions and accompanying transports would support other invasions. No ships larger than the light cruisers leading the destroyers were committed.

Air support would be provided by the 11th Koku Kantai, although one of its three Koku Sentai would be committed to operations in the Gulf of Thailand and South China Sea. Even the aircraft actually committed to the Philippines could remain no more than a month. After that they were needed elsewhere.

Japanese planners believed these forces, small as they were, sufficed. Prewar intelligence assessments set the US garrison at 22,000 troops, of which 6,500 were Filipino. US air forces were believed to total 180 aircraft, with 130 fighters, 30 bombers, and 20 naval patrol craft (a total larger than the 150 modern aircraft actually present). It overestimated the effective fighters and underestimated the available B-17s. The PAAC and the Philippine Army forces (as opposed to Philippine Scout units embedded in the US Philippine Division) were disregarded as militarily ineffective.

Japan believed it had several advantages. Amphibious invasion was a well-practiced activity for Japan. By 1941 Japan had launched similar-sized invasions up and down China's coast. The Imperial Army and Navy were well-practiced after four years of joint operations. Each side knew what was expected of it and what was needed to provide to the other service.

Lieutenant General Homma Masaharu commanded the Japanese 14th Army, which invaded the Philippines in December 1941. Known as "the Poet General" he proved better suited to an administrative command than a combat posting. (AC)

Conducting a combined arms offensive, with ground troops advancing under cover of air support was also well practiced by the Imperial Army. The IJAAS was almost entirely a tactical air service, intended to support Imperial Army ground forces. It knew how to gain air superiority and use command of the air to enable its bombers to isolate the battlefield and provide advancing troops fire support. It would isolate the battlefield by attacking supply lines, and rear area support installations (including artillery positions and airfields), but had no interest in strategic bombing. The Imperial Army believed air forces won wars by supporting ground forces on and behind the battlefield.

The IJNAS focus was different. It was intended to support the Imperial Navy's ability to project seapower, of which carrier air was the most obvious manifestation. However, the Imperial Navy also maintained land-based multi-engine *rikko* squadrons. Their crews were trained in both horizontal and torpedo bombing. They were equally skilled at attacking ships and land targets such as ports and airfields. They could attack targets as far as 750 miles from their base, escorted by Imperial Navy fighters, giving them a long reach lacked by the Imperial Army.

The capabilities of the two air services were complementary. The IJAAS could concentrate on near targets, directly supporting a landing or troops ashore. The IJNAS struck the distant targets, enemy airfields which could be used to oppose the Imperial Army efforts. It gave Japan a coordinated one–two punch yielding total control of the sky when successfully executed.

Both the importance of airpower and the Japanese military doctrine was underscored by Japan's invasion objectives and their order. Luzon, the Philippines's northern large island, was both physically its largest and its most important. It held the Philippines's largest city, capital, and major port, Manila. It was the most populous and the most developed island in the archipelago. It contained most of the islands' military installations and all its coastal forts. It also contained the Philippines's finest harbor, Manila Bay. Taking Luzon was key to conquering the Philippines.

While there were several beaches suitable for landings in Luzon, the best was at Lingayen Bay, on Luzon's northwest corner. It was a large, sheltered bay, and, once ashore there, an army could move down some of Luzon's best roads to Manila. A vast plain between Lingayen and Manila offered easy access between the two. Yet although Japan intended to make its main landing at Lingayen, near the port of Dagupan, it would not be the first spot invaded.

**OPPOSITE** US FERRY AND EVACUATION ROUTES TO AND FROM THE PHILIPPINES

Japan centered its operational plans around capturing territory containing an airfield or suitable for constructing one. Its first landing, the day the war began, was to secure an airfield on Batan Island, just north of Luzon. Aircraft there could provide air cover for future invasions. (NARA)

Four landings affecting Luzon would proceed it. On the war's opening day, a landing was planned for Batan Island, a small island just north of Luzon. Two days later, landings were scheduled at Vigan and Aparri, on Luzon's north coast. Two days after that, a Japanese force would land at Legaspi, in southeast Luzon. All objectives were either undefended or lightly defended. The primary goal at all four was to obtain an airfield. An airfield would be constructed at Batan. Civilian airfields at Vigan, Aparri, and Legaspi would be seized. Once secured, IJAAS fighters and light bombers would operate from them.

The northern airfields would provide air support for the Lingayen landing. Legaspi would provide an air umbrella for land forces to open a southern, second front against Manila from Lamon Bay. Only after its aircraft were operating on Luzon would the Imperial Army land its invasion forces at Lingayen and Lamon Bay, enveloping Manila in a pincer movement.

The IJNAS objective during this period was to overwhelm and destroy the US and Filipino air forces through deep strikes at their airfields. Once this was achieved, it would attack US Naval facilities in Luzon, forcing the US Navy out of the Philippines.

Nor were the remainder of the Philippines neglected. Landings at Davao on the large southern Philippine island of Mindanao were planned for December 20 and landings on Jolo, an island at the archipelago's southwestern quadrant were planned for December 25. In both cases the objective was to seize the local airfield. Japanese aircraft would be ferried there later to support a future ground offensive. Airpower remained the key to the Japanese offensive.

## United States' objectives

The US did not really want the Philippines. It took them as spoils after the 1898 Spanish–American War, when it captured the islands. Nineteenth-century prestige meant the US had to keep the Spanish colony, but it proved a sink for both blood and treasure ever since. Despite the English writer Rudyard Kipling's famous colonialist challenge, the US had been looking to lay down "the white man's burden" since shortly after taking the islands.

Although the US was historically an expansionist nation, it was not a colonial one. Any land it took, it intended to become part of the US, with eventual admission to statehood

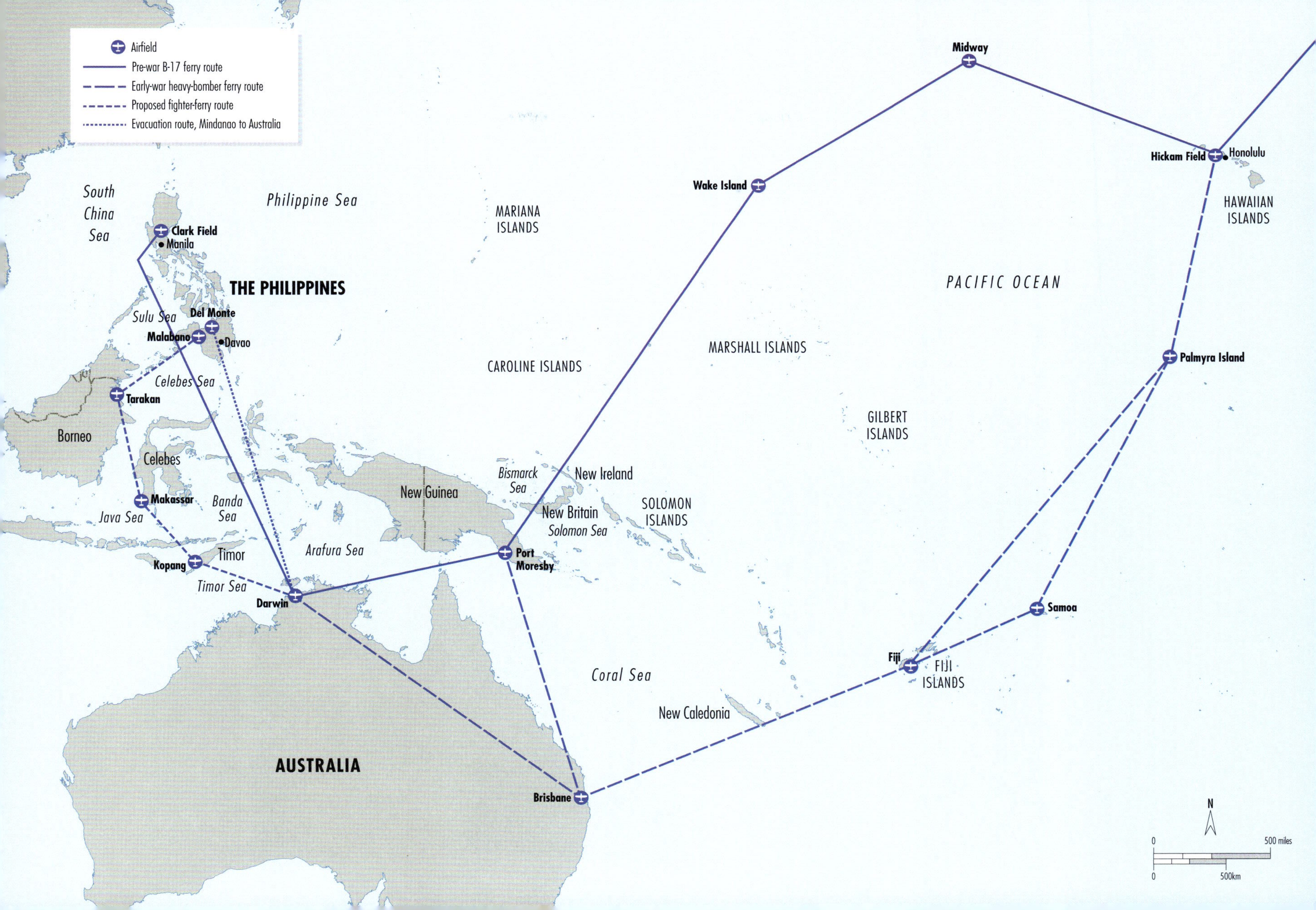

Airfield
Pre-war B-17 ferry route
Early-war heavy-bomber ferry route
Proposed fighter-ferry route
Evacuation route, Mindanao to Australia
South China Sea
Philippine Sea
Clark Field
Manila
THE PHILIPPINES
Sulu Sea
Del Monte
Malabano
Davao
Celebes Sea
Tarakan
Borneo
Celebes
Makassar
Java Sea
Banda Sea
Timor
Kopang
Timor Sea
Darwin
Arafura Sea
New Guinea
Bismarck Sea
New Ireland
New Britain
Solomon Sea
SOLOMON ISLANDS
Port Moresby
Coral Sea
New Caledonia
AUSTRALIA
Brisbane
MARIANA ISLANDS
CAROLINE ISLANDS
MARSHALL ISLANDS
GILBERT ISLANDS
Wake Island
Midway
Hickam Field
Honolulu
HAWAIIAN ISLANDS
PACIFIC OCEAN
Palmyra Island
Samoa
Fiji
FIJI ISLANDS
N
0
500 miles
0
500km

**OPPOSITE** US AND PHILIPPINE AIRFIELDS 1941

After annexing the Philippines in 1898, the US soon realized it did not really want it. After over a decade of effort, the Philippines were put on a path to independence in 1946 when President Roosevelt signed the Philippine Independence Bill in 1934. (LOC)

after it became a largely white, English-speaking, Judeo-Christian polity. It followed this policy in Louisiana (formerly French), Florida (Spanish), the American Southwest (seized from Mexico), and all Native American lands. There was an implicit assumption that those originally there would eventually assimilate into the American culture.

This was a big reason the US never considered annexing Cuba. It was considered a poor candidate for assimilation. The smaller, less populated Puerto Rico was considered a better candidate. Alaska was virtually unpopulated, while Hawaii, Guam, and American Samoa were viewed as strategically important islands with small populations.

The distant Philippines were never believed a good candidate for assimilation into the United States. Originally ruled as conquered foreign territory, the 1902 Philippine Organic Act made the Philippines an unincorporated territory where the US Constitution did not fully apply because they were occupied by "alien races." The US spent the next three decades trying to hand over more local autonomy to the Filipinos native to the islands, under benevolent (in the US's view) supervision of the US.

In 1934, tired of both the philosophical contradictions in, and the expense of, maintaining a foreign colony, the US Congress passed the Philippine Independence Act, or Tydings–McDuffie Act. It established the Philippines as a commonwealth, requiring it to establish a constitution, consistent with the rights and liberties accorded by the US Constitution. Ten years after the Philippine constitution was approved by the US, the Philippines would achieve independence.

Yet although the US was leaving, strategic considerations required the US guarantee Philippine independence. The US could not permit a foreign power to occupy the colony. The Philippines dominated communications routes between the US West Coast and the Far East. China, Indochina, and the Dutch East Indies were important trading partners. The US intended to guarantee Philippine independence through a defensive alliance and by standing up a Philippine army capable of defending the archipelago.

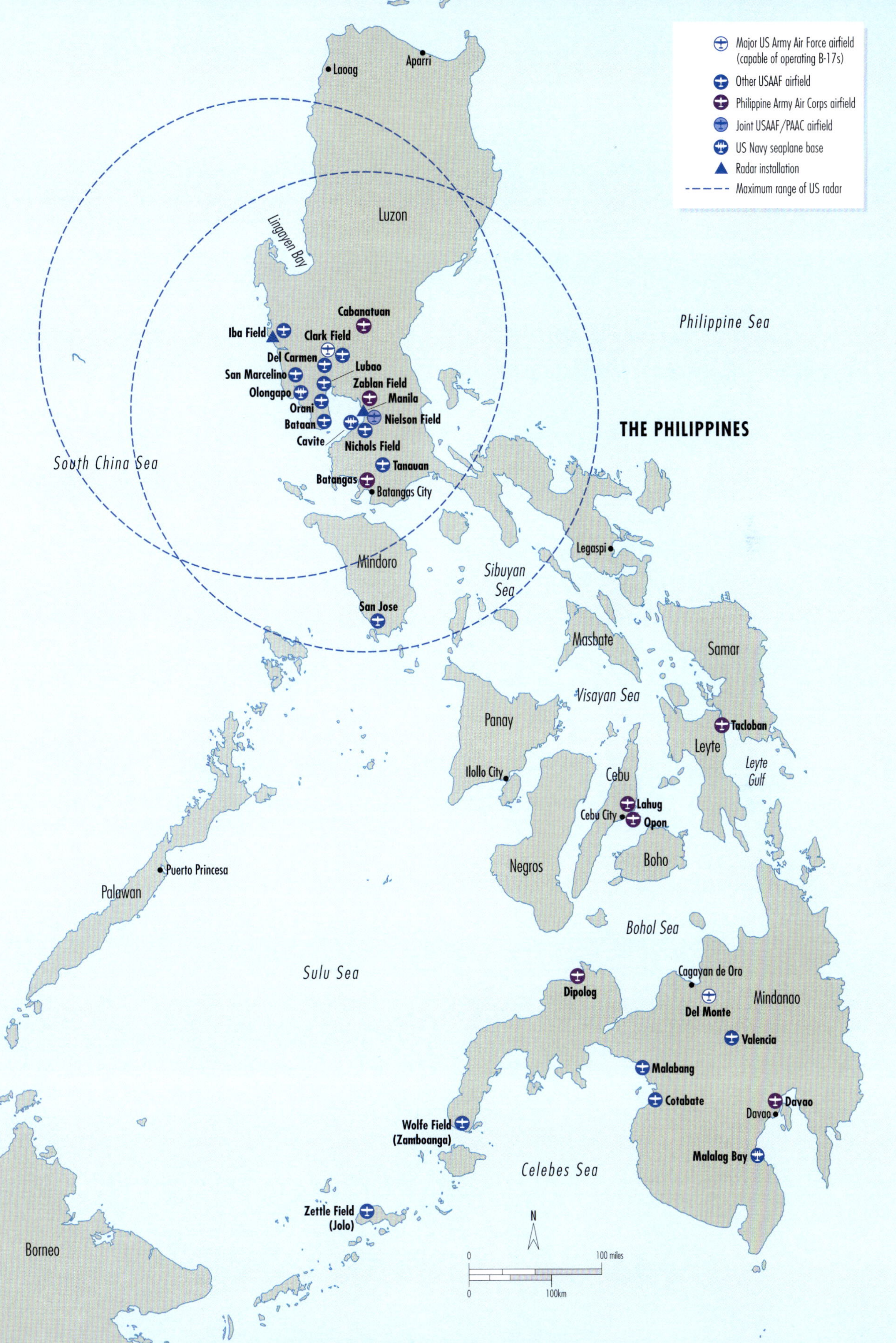

Major US Army Air Force airfield (capable of operating B-17s)
Other USAAF airfield
Philippine Army Air Corps airfield
Joint USAAF/PAAC airfield
US Navy seaplane base
Radar installation
Maximum range of US radar
THE PHILIPPINES
Laoag
Aparri
Luzon
Lingayen Bay
Philippine Sea
Cabanatuan
Iba Field
Clark Field
Del Carmen
Lubao
San Marcelino
Zablan Field
Olongapo
Manila
Orani
Nielson Field
Bataan
Cavite
Nichols Field
South China Sea
Tanauan
Batangas
Batangas City
Legaspi
Mindoro
Sibuyan Sea
San Jose
Masbate
Samar
Visayan Sea
Panay
Tacloban
Leyte
Leyte Gulf
Ilollo City
Cebu
Lahug
Cebu City
Opon
Boho
Negros
Puerto Princesa
Palawan
Bohol Sea
Sulu Sea
Dipolog
Cagayan de Oro
Del Monte
Mindanao
Valencia
Malabang
Cotabate
Davao
Davao
Wolfe Field (Zamboanga)
Malalag Bay
Celebes Sea
Zettle Field (Jolo)
N
Borneo
0
100 miles
0
100km

This made the US's strategic goal thereafter one of military disengagement. It wanted to extricate itself from further Philippine entanglement. It did not want to leave the Philippines a target for other powers in the area, whether European or Japanese. It wanted an independent Philippines which would serve as a trading partner and potential future ally. Part of the reason for the decade-long transition was to let the Philippines develop a robust military. Additionally, the US planned a military alliance with the new nation. Washington planners felt this combination would encourage regional bullies to look elsewhere.

The plan was for the Philippines to develop an army of ten infantry divisions and its own air force. The infantry divisions would be light infantry, with only 75mm artillery in its divisional field artillery regiment. While the US intended to pull most of its military out of the Philippines after independence, it intended to backstop the newly independent government. The US Navy would secure the waters around the Commonwealth, while the US Army Air Forces would be available for air support.

One fallout from this decision was the US had little motivation to improve and modernize its own military infrastructure in the Philippines after 1936. It built extensive coastal fortifications to protect Manila Bay between 1905 and 1919, but the Washington Naval Limitations Treaty of 1922 put a 13-year moratorium on further fortification, expiring at the end of 1935. Since they were losing their army and naval facilities after 1946, the US saw no reason to modernize fortifications and facilities. The Philippine government was expected to build their own training bases, while the US would maintain their own already existing facilities until handover.

The exception was airfields. Since the US saw a significant role for US airpower as part of their commitment to protect the Philippines, it had an interest in seeing adequate airfields existed. In the late 1930s airfield construction was inexpensive. Grass fields sufficed for single-engine warplanes, and macadamized runways were good enough for multi-engine aircraft. One-story and two-story frame buildings suited hangars, workshops, mess halls, and barracks. The US began improving and adding airfields in the late 1930s.

In 1935 the Philippine government brought in Douglas MacArthur, who was retiring from his position as US Army Chief of Staff, to train this new army. Although MacArthur arrived in 1936, training did not start until 1937. Even then, only one-fifth the number needed for the army was inducted. Similarly, the first Philippine Army Air Corps squadron was organized in 1939. Philippine forces were outfitted with US castoffs, including rifles from the 19th century and aircraft discarded by the US Army Air Corps.

By 1940 it was obvious Japan was the most likely US opponent in the Pacific. The US had been planning for war against Japan since the early 1900s. That plan called for US forces on Luzon to fall back to the Bataan Peninsula and await relief. The peninsula was protected by a series of coastal defense fortifications preventing attack from the sea. Ammunition, food, and supplies stored in Bataan permitted forces there to hold out for a minimum of a year. Updated throughout the 1920s and 1930s, the plan had the advantage of minimizing US peacetime commitments in the Philippines.

MacArthur scrapped this plan when he took command of the Philippine Army. He viewed it as too defensive, since it failed to use the new Philippine Army. He chose to defend the Philippines at the beaches, placing the units where they could immediately counterattack the Japanese when they landed. Stores formerly kept on Bataan were moved behind Lingayen, where they could resupply the Filipino and US forces attacking the invaders.

Washington liked the new approach. If successful it meant the US would hold on to its major Luzon airfields: Clark Field, Nielson Field, and Nichols Field. Airstrips could be built on Bataan, but they were rudimentary. Keeping the maintenance and logistics capabilities of the established airfields would allow the Far Eastern Air Forces to perform more efficiently.

From Washington, it seemed plausible. The US Philippine Division was viewed as a match for any two Japanese divisions, and it would be backed up by seven Philippine Army

As part of the preparation for Philippine independence, the US helped the Commonwealth to form its own army, including a Philippine Army Air Corps. On August 17, 1941, with war tensions growing, a ceremony was held at Camp Murphy, Rizal to mark the induction of the PAAC into the US Army Air Forces. (AC)

divisions, three of which were stationed near the likely invasion beaches. Since the airbases would be held, this ground force could be supported by nearby USAAF units, the fighters providing air cover and the bombers interdicting the invading troops. US intelligence rated Japan's aerial capabilities as well below that of the US.

Everything was based on faulty assumptions. The Philippine Division was understrength. The Philippine Army, including the divisions designated to defend the beaches, were untrained and ill-equipped. They lacked artillery, communications, transportation, and antiaircraft support. Their officers were inexperienced. Units barely able to hold a prepared, fixed position were being asked to conduct a mobile offensive. Regardless, it became the policy the US followed to achieve its objective of holding the Philippines.

As with the Japanese, the US emphasized airpower's role in its plans. Starting in January 1941, the US Army Air Forces began reinforcing the air garrison in the Philippines. This included replacing the fighters of the existing fighter wing in the Philippines with modern P-40E aircraft and sending three bomber and one fighter wing to the Philippines. Two of the bomber wings had B-17 heavy bombers; the third consisted of A-24s, the Army version of the Douglas Dauntless dive bomber.

The task and purpose of these aircraft was less clear. They were to defend the Philippines (except for the A-24s which had not yet arrived when the war started), which was a clear tactical mission, but exactly how that objective was to be achieved was poorly defined. The fighters were presumably to intercept any enemy aircraft attacking the Philippines, but to be effective this required an early warning system which did not exist and had to be created.

The role of the B-17s was even murkier. The USAAF was committing the majority of its B-17s to defend the Philippines, without defining their mission. They were powerful long-range bombers envisioned for strategic bombardment of industry. Presumably they could be used to knock out Japanese airfields in Formosa (or Indochina), but this worked best as a first strike. The US was not ready to conduct this type of preemptive action, nor had the FEAF conducted prewar planning for such strikes.

They could be used for maritime patrol and antishipping as the RAF did. (The name "Flying Fortress" came from the claim they would serve as mobile coastal fortresses to protect the American coasts.) However, to be effective in that role crews had to be trained for it, training the crews sent to the Philippines lacked. It is hard to avoid the conclusion their main objective was to overawe Japan into avoiding war with the US. The result was to be expected, and this scarecrow strategy failed.

# THE CAMPAIGN

The Clark Field air raids concluding with A6M Zeros from the 23rd Koku Sentai strafing the airfields. They spent nearly 30 minutes working over the airfields, concentrating on parked aircraft and vehicles. (AC)

In July 1941 Japan decided to go to war with the United States, Great Britain, and the Netherlands. They were the three great colonial powers opposing Japan's war with China. All had resources badly needed by Japan's war machine: rubber, tin, aluminum, and especially petroleum. Japan occupied Tonkin in September 1940, and the US embargoed scrap iron and steel sales to Japan following that. Japan then negotiated a treaty with Vichy France allowing Japanese occupation of all French Indochina in July 1941. On July 26, 1941 the US instituted a total petroleum embargo on Japan, and convinced the Dutch and British to follow suit.

This gave Japan until March 1942 before its economy – and armed forces – ground to a halt. Japan produced very little oil domestically, importing most of it, but it had choices. It could either accede to US demands or go to war to seize the resources it needed. The US oilfields were safely distant from Japanese incursion; those of Britain and the Netherlands were within striking distance of the Indochina bases Japan had just acquired. Japan laid plans to seize the oilfields, while simultaneously establishing a defensive perimeter to protect its gains.

While Japan conducted political negotiations to lift the embargo, it found the terms offered by the US unacceptable. The US was not just demanding Japan exit Indochina, but wanted Japan to leave the territory they had taken from China. The Japanese interpreted it as being told to exit all the lands it had conquered since 1931. Japan rejected this.

While the US believed a war was likely, it also believed initial US involvement would be limited to the Philippines. It updated prewar war plans involving Japan and studied ways in which the US Army and Navy would battle across the Pacific to relieve the Philippines. It started rushing reinforcements in January 1941, but the planned buildup would not be complete for over a year.

When the war started, all prewar planning became obsolete. The Japanese attack on Pearl Harbor crippled the US Pacific Fleet. The Japanese offensive in the Central Pacific was more aggressive than expected. The Philippines were on their own. Worse, many reinforcements had not yet arrived, including many of the aircraft and the air warning battalion being sent. US and Philippine preparations had been dilatory. Five radar sets awaited deployment, and work had just begun on the Mindanao airfields.

Japan imported 80 percent of its petroleum from the United States aboard tankers like *Tao Maru*, shown here at San Pedro, California. Japan had to agree to US demands or make up the shortfall by seizing oilfields next to the South China Sea by force. Their choice to seize them ignited war. (USNHHC)

By contrast, Japanese plans were disciplined, economical, and realistic. They conducted a complex set of invasion operations, leading with their air forces. They quickly seized command of the air, and used that to operate inside the decision loop of their US opponents. The Japanese moved faster than their opponents could react, attacking simultaneously at different places. The campaign that followed was decided in the first week of the war, largely over in the first month, and from an aerial perspective was a mopping up operation through early May 1942.

## Build up – September 26, 1940 to December 7, 1941

When September 1940 began, neither the US nor Japan seriously expected war with the other. Japan's occupation of Tonkin on September 26, 1940, followed by their signing the Axis Tripartite Pact on the following day, forced the US to realistically consider the possibility. Similarly, Japan began updating its war plans against the United States, including preparations for invading the Philippines.

In September 1940 the US in the Philippines was in worse shape than the Japanese in Formosa, from which any invasion of the archipelago was expected to come. They had never had top priority among US outposts and US war planners long believed the Philippines could not be profitably defended against a determined Japanese assault with available forces there. The US Army Air Corps (it became the US Army Air Forces on June 20, 1941) garrison was little more than a token, a pawn to be removed from the board at the first exchange. By summer 1940, the Air Corps contingent consisted of a dozen B-10 bombers, 28 P-26 fighters, three B-18 bombers, and a collection of trainers allocated to the PAAC. The US Navy had one squadron of 14 PBY-4s, VP-21, sent in September 1939.

Japan was in much better shape. The 11th Koku Kantai was headquartered in Takao, although at this time they were stationed to support operations against China. Similarly,

Worried about Japanese aggression USAAF command began moving warplanes to the Philippines starting in early 1941. The reinforcements sent were a mix bag of whatever was available, including B-18 bombers. (USNHHC)

while the Imperial Army had the 5th Hikoshidan in Formosa, it was concentrating against China, as were the ground forces eventually assigned to the 1941 invasion of the Philippines. The resources they would eventually use were available. They just had to be re-tasked.

The US buildup began before the Japanese, drastically altered after Japan occupied Tonkin. In October, 48 Seversky P-35s were ordered sent to the Philippines. The fighters, diverted from a shipment originally to be sent to Sweden, were mediocre but available. The aircraft arrived November 1940, and two squadrons of P-35s were activated on November 17.

Realizing this was inadequate, the Army Air Corps sent more aircraft in early 1941. Eighteen B-18s were crated up and sent by ship in March, followed by 31 P-40Bs in April. By May these had arrived. On May 6, 1941, two new fighter squadrons became operational at Nichols Field and a bomber squadron at Clark Field.

It took Japan's total occupation of Indochina to accelerate activity. Concurrent with the imposition of the oil embargo, US Army headquarters in Washington nationalized the Philippine Army, merging it with the US Army in the Philippines. It recalled Douglas MacArthur, then a field marshal in the Philippine Army, to active duty as a lieutenant general. It was a two-star drop in rank, but as he was given command of the new US Army in the Far East, it represented an increase in power and prestige. On November 16, 1941, the Philippine Department Air Force was reorganized into the Far East Air Force.

Washington also began a dramatic increase in units sent to the Philippines, both land and air. It believed if the US air forces in the Philippines were large enough, especially if enough heavy B-17 bombers were sent, the force would "act as a threat to keep Japan in line." Preparation began to send four heavy bombardment groups, 272 B-17s, and two additional fighter groups, 130 P-40Es, to the Philippines.

The first tranche was sent in 1941. Fifty P-40Es were sent directly from the factory to the Philippines as they came off the assembly line. Twenty-eight P-40Bs were reassigned from existing units stateside. Both were sent in September.

Through 1939 Army Air Corps aircraft could fly no more than 100 miles from the coasts of the United States. In 1941 its pilots had almost no long-range overwater experience.

Yet the only way to get B-17s to the Philippines was to fly them. The US Navy stepped in to help. Runways at navy airfields on Midway and Wake Island were hastily improved to take B-17s in July and August.

Guam was ruled out as a stopover because it was in the middle of Japanese-controlled territory. Instead, a route through Australia was selected. The US Navy flew two USAAF officers to get Australian permission to use Australian airfields and conduct a survey to determine which airfields were suitable.

By September the first flight was conducted. Nine B-17Ds were flown to the Philippines from Hawaii. After stops at Midway and Wake, the bombers flew to Port Moresby in Australian New Guinea. Since the route took them over Japanese Mandate islands, to avoid

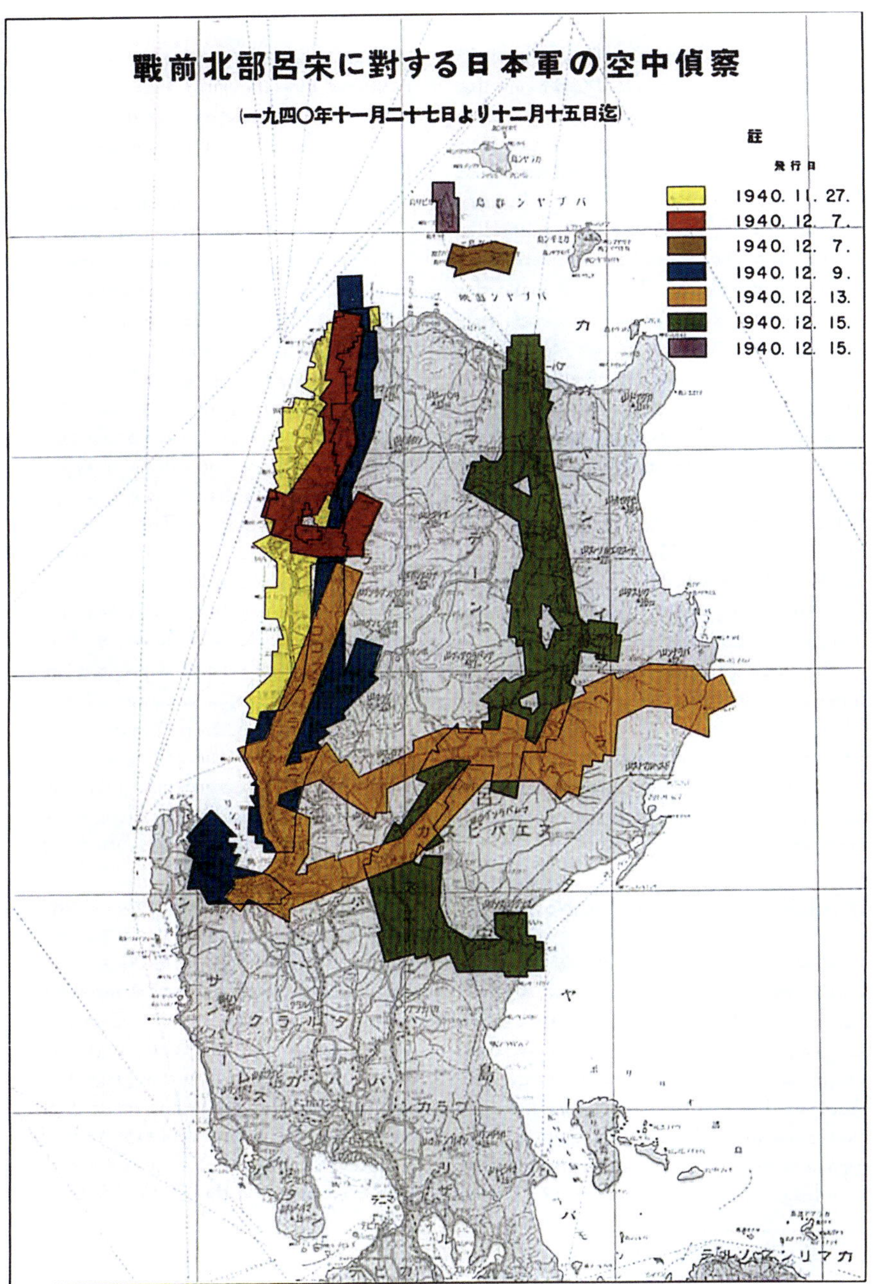


Between November 27 and December 15, 1940 Japan flew seven clandestine photoreconnaissance missions over northern Luzon. They used commercial airliners for the flights. The area captured is shown in this map. (AC)

detection that leg was flown at night and at 21,000ft instead of 8,000ft. From there they flew to Darwin, Australia, and to Clark Field from Darwin. The flight took over a week, but they were not detected by Japan. More flights followed and by the end of November there were 36 B-17s in the Philippines. Another 36 were on the way, interrupted by the outbreak of the war. One flight arrived as Pearl Harbor was being attacked.

A southern route was developed. It ran from Christmas Island (today's Kiritimati Atoll) to Canton Island, and from there to either Fiji or American Samoa. From there aircraft flew to Free French New Caledonia, Brisbane, and Darwin. Permissions were obtained by mid-November, with the route to open January 15, 1942. This, too, became moot after the war began. It was used instead as a ferry route to Australia.

The Army further accelerated reinforcements during autumn. The Air Force Chief of Staff appointed a new air commander to the Philippines in October 1941, General Lewis Brereton. In Florida when appointed, Brereton did not reach the Philippines until November 3, 1941. He spent his first week familiarizing himself with his command, then spent the rest of the month in Australia, developing the southern ferry route. He was not able to turn his attention to his command until November 30, the day he received the warning that a war with Japan was imminent.

Army Air Forces command also dispatched 52 A-24 dive bombers to the Philippines, and 18 P-40Es for another fighter squadron, cutting orders for their transfer in October, and intending to have them operational by mid-November. The Army also began the transfer of two infantry and one artillery regiment to beef up the ground garrison.

By November, the situation deteriorated so much that Washington was unwilling to send anything by ship to the Philippines without naval escort, delaying the transfers. The convoy finally departed California on November 21, carrying the A-24s, a squadron of P-40Es, the ground elements of a second B-17 group, and a field artillery brigade. It also carried P-40Es intended for the American Volunteer Group in China. It was still at sea when the war started.

The US Navy beefed up its aerial contingent, transferring a second PBY squadron to the Philippines. The unit arrived in early December, days before the war began. The units were renumbered as VP-101 and VP-102, and merged into Patrol Wing 10. One squadron operated out of Olongapo, with the second stationed at Cavite's Sangley Point seaplane base.

Japanese preparations to invade the Philippines were not as fraught as US preparations to defend them, especially air resources. These were already on hand in Formosa. There were significant aviation resources in Formosa or close at hand when Japan began planning its offensive. It transferred the Imperial Army 3rd Hikoshidan from China to Indochina and one Koku Sentai of Imperial Japanese Navy Air Force's 11th Koku Kantai from Formosa to Indochina to support operations against the British and Dutch.

The first active preparations began over a year before the war started. Between November 27 and December 15, 1940 Japan conducted seven photographic reconnaissance missions over Northern Luzon. They were flown using commercial Nippon Airways airliners, equipped with cameras. They were manned by military pilots and observers. Flights were made at 21,000ft, and except at the southernmost point were beyond range of detection by US forces.

Coverage extended over the east coast of Luzon from Caparispisan to Lingayen Bay, Aparri to Baler Bay, across Luzon from Baler to Lingayen Bay and the Babuyan islands of Dalupiri and Fuga. These flights avoided Clark Field and stayed north of Dingalan Bay. The Japanese gained no aerial photo intelligence about Clark Field, Bataan, the airfield at Iba, Manila Bay, Manila, and Lamon Bay. Yet it achieved the goal of scouting out the territory around Aparri, Vigan, and Lingayen Bay, where the first landings were scheduled.

Once the decision to go to war was made, following the US-led petroleum embargo on July 26, 1941, Japanese land units assigned to the invasion of the Philippines conducted

Once Japan decided to go to war, it initiated preparations, moving units to jumping-off points. It also initiated realistic training maneuvers. Units participating in landings conducted landing exercises in the months before the war opened. (AC)

intensive amphibious operations and jungle warfare training along the South China coast and training areas near Canton and Hainan Island.

On November 6, 1941 Japan put their war plan into motion, with an initial start date for the war of December 1 (Sunday November 30 in Hawaii). It was pushed forward one week to December 8, but with that decision pre-invasion preparations began. Ground forces for the invasion moved to their departure ports – Japan dispersed the departure ports to avoid large concentrations of shipping detectable by aerial reconnaissance or spies on the ground. Main Force units moved to Takao and Keelung in Formosa or Mako in the Pescadores. The units landing at Lamon Bay gathered at Amami Ōshima, in the Ryukyu Islands, while those slated to land on Mindanao moved to Palau.

These consisted of the 48th and 16th Infantry Divisions reinforced by two tank regiments and ten artillery battalions, commanded by General Homma Masaharu. From the perspective of the air campaign, they were accompanied by five antiaircraft battalions and several engineering battalions specializing in repairing and building airfields. All moved to debarkation ports starting November 20.

Events were building to a head as both sides prepared for war. The US War Department sent Army dependents home from the Philippines by May 1941. The Navy joined suit later, sending dependents home in November. After July, the Army Air Force began dispersing fighter squadrons to alternate airfields, Iba, Del Carmen, and San Marcelino in Luzon being chief among these. Worried about the vulnerability of Clark Field to attack from Formosa, Far East Air Force Command decided a second B-17 airfield, out of range of Formosa, was needed. Del Monte in Mindanao was expanded, with the B-17s to be transferred there. Available in November, half the B-17s were moved there, with the rest to follow in mid-December.

Readiness, at least on the US side, was hampered by a lack of spare parts and suitable facilities. There were no spare parts or spare engines available, a situation created by a general lack of spare parts ordered in 1940. Even tools were in short supply, and a needed depot expansion had not occurred. Radar specialists arrived in the fall to train operators, but there were no facilities for training available.

Worried about the exposure of Clark Field to Japanese attack FEAF command decided to build a B-17 airfield on Mindanao. Work started in November and half the B-17s were transferred there in the first week of December. At that point most of its facilities were housed in canvas tents. (NARA)

Both sides increased readiness and aerial reconnaissance during October and November. US Interceptor Command was placed on 24-hour operations. (The Japanese air forces were already there.) Both navies, Japanese and US, had increased aerial patrolling in October, essentially going to a war footing. Instead of conducting multiple-PBY training patrols, PBYs were sent on individual war patrols, covering the South China Sea to the Indochina and China coasts.

Starting September, they were also sent out armed, with instructions to shoot at any German surface raiders spotted on sight. There were no German surface raiders then near the Philippines and the US was still at peace with the Germans. The PBY crews took it as tacit permission to attack the Japanese.

Starting November, the PBYs were dispersed to advance bases. Three with the tender *William B. Preston* were sent to Davao. *Heron*, with four single-engine floatplanes, was sent to Palawan to cover the approaches to the Celebes Sea. The rest in Cavite and Olongapo patrolled the South China Sea in an arc running from the coast of Indochina to Formosa. Nothing unusual was spotted through December 1.

On December 2 things started moving. Patrolling PBYs spotted 20 cargo ships and transports in Cam Ranh Bay. The Navy increased patrols west of Luzon, asking General Brereton to cover the area between Luzon and Formosa. The next day, 50 ships, including warships were seen there. On December 3 they were gone, departed for the Dutch East Indies and Malaya. Admiral Hart, commanding the US Asiatic Fleet, ordered all major US Navy warships, to depart Luzon, taking station outside Japanese air range.

Starting December 4, the Japanese aircraft began making familiarization flights from Luzon, flying formations of nine to 27 aircraft to within 20 miles of Lingayen Bay. These flights were detected by the Iba radar station. US Army fighters began night patrols,

The first Japanese attack on the Philippines hit Mindanao, not Luzon. While Japanese aircraft in Formosa were fogged in, carrier aircraft attacked Davao. They found seaplane tender *William B. Preston* and two of its three PBYs anchored in the harbor and attacked. The PBYs were destroyed, but *Preston* forced down one bomber. (AC)

and on successive nights, intercepted Japanese formations, which turned back short of Philippine airspace.

Patrolling PBYs and Japanese G3Ms encountered each other on December 4–7 as Japan stepped up its air activities. No shots were exchanged, but on December 7 a G3M attempted to work itself into a firing position behind a PBY. Skilled flying by the PBY's pilot denied the Japanese bomber a firing opportunity. Despite these ominous developments a peacetime tempo continued among the US forces.

Despite last-ditch diplomatic maneuvering seeking a negotiated settlement, Japan decided to go to war on December 8 (in the Philippines). On December 6, 1941 (in Tokyo) Imperial General Headquarters decided to direct Japan's ambassador to the US to deliver a note ending Japanese–American negotiations and declaring war at 1300hrs Washington, D.C. time. The Pearl Harbor attack was scheduled to begin 30 minutes later at 0730hrs Hawaiian time. In the meantime, three convoys carrying troops scheduled to land at Batan Island, Aparri, and Vigan were already at sea, having departed Formosa on December 7. The first actions of the land war would secure airfields at those sites. The war was about to begin.

## Opening day – December 8, 1941

At 0755hrs on December 7, 1941 Hawaiian time, the first Japanese bomb fell on Pearl Harbor, opening the Pacific War. It was 1355hrs in Washington, D.C; 25 minutes after Japan's Ambassador Nomura, delayed by decoding problems, arrived at the State Department at 1405hrs and presented Japan's declaration of war at 1420hrs, nearly one hour late.

It was 0155hrs on December 8 in Manila and 1255hrs in Tokyo (the Imperial Military used Tokyo time) when the attack began. Manila first learned of the attack, and the implied state of war, between 0200hrs and 0330hrs Manila time. It was unofficial.

General Sutherland, MacArthur's chief of staff heard it on commercial broadcasts at 0330hrs. He passed the word to MacArthur and notified all Army commanders a state

## AIR ACTIVITY, DECEMBER 8, 1941

of war existed with Japan. The Navy's duty operator intercepted the "Air raid on Pearl Harbor. This is no drill" message sent by a radio operator there when the attack occurred. He recognized the sender's technique, notifying Admiral Hart. Hart signaled the US Navy, "Japan started hostilities. Govern yourself accordingly." Official confirmation came at 0500hrs, but US forces in the Philippines already knew they were at war.

Radar at Iba detected a large flight of Japanese aircraft inbound from Formosa, estimated at 75 aircraft, at 0330hrs. P-40Es were sent to intercept them, but failed to make contact, even when radar showed the two groups of aircraft had met. Army pilots apparently flew under the Japanese formation, which swung west and was lost to radar.

Active hostilities began at dawn, but not in the air over Luzon. Japanese forces landed at Batan Island. The undefended Batan Island was quickly subjugated by a 490-man naval landing unit sent there. A small airstrip at Basco was seized. Elements of the Imperial Army's 24th Airfield Battalion examined it, deciding it could be used by single-engine warplanes, but required expansion for full-scale operations. It was available by the end of the day. The Imperial Army had a usable fighter field only 30 miles from Luzon.

Davao, in Mindanao, was the first Philippine town attacked by Japanese aircraft. At dawn on December 8, 21 aircraft from the carrier *Ryujo* attacked the port. Seaplane tender *William B. Preston* and three PBYs were there. One PBY was on patrol. The other two were destroyed at their moorings by the Japanese aircraft. *Preston* shot down one Aichi D3A dive bomber. Undamaged by the attack, *Preston* cleared the harbor to seek a safer anchorage. The patrolling PBY, airborne when *Preston* departed Davao, was instructed to go to Polloc Harbor near Parang on Mindanao's west coast.

While the four PBYs with *Heron* at Palawan had an uneventful day, the PBYs at Cavite and Olongapo prepared for war. At each base they were split into attack and patrol groups. At Olongapo seven PBYs were designated a scouting group, while seven, sent to *Childs* in Manila Bay, were held back as an attack group. At Cavite four became the scouting group and five, sent to Laguna del Bay, 80 miles south of Manila, became the attack group, held in reserve until targets appeared. All were armed with four 500lb bombs each and training machine-gun ammunition. No other machine-gun ammunition was available.

Scouting patrols began at 0600hrs, but the South China Sea areas searched, west and northwest of Luzon, were empty of Japanese ships on December 8. At 1000hrs, one of the

Japan intended a dawn strike at US airfields and installations in Luzon on December 8, but their aircraft were fogged in at their Fomosan airfields that morning. Only a handful of Imperial Army bombers were able to take off at the scheduled time. (AC)

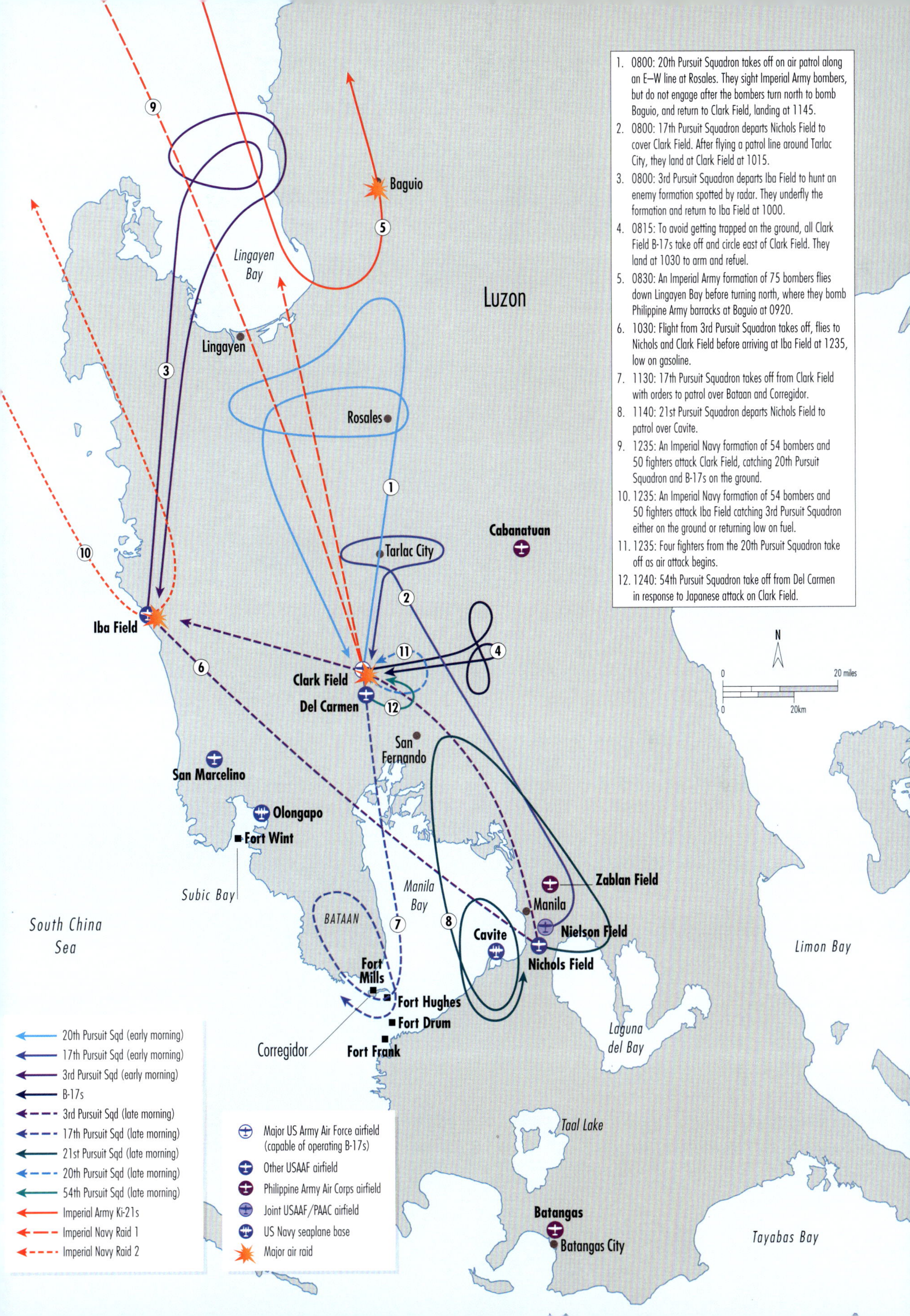
1. 0800: 20th Pursuit Squadron takes off on air patrol along an E–W line at Rosales. They sight Imperial Army bombers, but do not engage after the bombers turn north to bomb Baguio, and return to Clark Field, landing at 1145.
2. 0800: 17th Pursuit Squadron departs Nichols Field to cover Clark Field. After flying a patrol line around Tarlac City, they land at Clark Field at 1015.
3. 0800: 3rd Pursuit Squadron departs Iba Field to hunt an enemy formation spotted by radar. They underfly the formation and return to Iba Field at 1000.
4. 0815: To avoid getting trapped on the ground, all Clark Field B-17s take off and circle east of Clark Field. They land at 1030 to arm and refuel.
5. 0830: An Imperial Army formation of 75 bombers flies down Lingayen Bay before turning north, where they bomb Philippine Army barracks at Baguio at 0920.
6. 1030: Flight from 3rd Pursuit Squadron takes off, flies to Nichols and Clark Field before arriving at Iba Field at 1235, low on gasoline.
7. 1130: 17th Pursuit Squadron takes off from Clark Field with orders to patrol over Bataan and Corregidor.
8. 1140: 21st Pursuit Squadron departs Nichols Field to patrol over Cavite.
9. 1235: An Imperial Navy formation of 54 bombers and 50 fighters attack Clark Field, catching 20th Pursuit Squadron and B-17s on the ground.
10. 1235: An Imperial Navy formation of 54 bombers and 50 fighters attack Iba Field catching 3rd Pursuit Squadron either on the ground or returning low on fuel.
11. 1235: Four fighters from the 20th Pursuit Squadron take off as air attack begins.
12. 1240: 54th Pursuit Squadron take off from Del Carmen in response to Japanese attack on Clark Field.
Baguio
Lingayen Bay
Lingayen
Luzon
Rosales
Cabanatuan
Tarlac City
Iba Field
Clark Field
Del Carmen
N
0
20 miles
0
20km
San Fernando
San Marcelino
Olongapo
Fort Wint
Subic Bay
Manila Bay
Zablan Field
Manila
Nielson Field
Nichols Field
Cavite
BATAAN
South China Sea
Fort Mills
Fort Hughes
Fort Drum
Fort Frank
Corregidor
Limon Bay
Laguna del Bay
Taal Lake
Batangas
Batangas City
Tayabas Bay
20th Pursuit Sqd (early morning)
17th Pursuit Sqd (early morning)
3rd Pursuit Sqd (early morning)
B-17s
3rd Pursuit Sqd (late morning)
17th Pursuit Sqd (late morning)
21st Pursuit Sqd (late morning)
20th Pursuit Sqd (late morning)
54th Pursuit Sqd (late morning)
Imperial Army Ki-21s
Imperial Navy Raid 1
Imperial Navy Raid 2
Major US Army Air Force airfield (capable of operating B-17s)
Other USAAF airfield
Philippine Army Air Corps airfield
Joint USAAF/PAAC airfield
US Navy seaplane base
Major air raid

patrolling PBYs was detached from duties to fly Rear Admiral William Glassford to his flagship, the heavy cruiser *Houston*, then at Iloilo Bay in the central Philippines.

The early morning air raids on Luzon planned by Japan and expected by the US never occurred. The Imperial Army and Navy aircraft were fueled and armed after receiving their notification of the Pearl Harbor attack, but the Japanese had planned to arrive over the Philippines at dawn, departing their airfields in Formosa two to three hours before that. At midnight, just as December 7 ended and December 8 arrived, dense fog rolled in, blanketing the southern half of the island. It was still there at dawn, preventing the scheduled launches.

Instead, they were stuck on the ground. Surprise was gone. Japanese commanders anticipated flying into a hornets' nest of waiting US fighters, alert and armed, defending Philippine skies. Worse, they feared the US had sent a counterstrike to hit Japan's Formosa airfields. It was an air commander's worst nightmare, getting caught on the ground, planes lined up to launch, armed and filled with gasoline. Japan, without radar, depended on visual observers for air warning. If the US bombers came in from the sea, the Japanese would get only minutes' warning before the US struck.

General Brereton was trying to realize Japan's worst nightmare. He had plans drawn up to attack Formosa airfields shortly after arrival but he lacked current photoreconnaissance, so sought permission to conduct reconnaissance over Formosa on December 4. MacArthur, seeking to avoid provoking the Japanese, denied the request. Regardless, plans existed and Brereton wanted to execute them. Just like his Japanese counterparts he feared having his bombers caught on the ground. Sending them to bomb the enemy's airfields guaranteed they would not be.

Brereton asked to speak to MacArthur at 0500hrs. Instead, Brereton spoke to Sutherland. Still in peacetime mode, Brereton asked permission to make a daylight raid on Formosa. Sutherland told Brereton to prepare for the raid, but not to launch it until obtaining MacArthur's authorization. Brereton, from his headquarters at Nielson Field, conferred with Colonel Eugene Eubank, commanding 5th Bomber Command, who arrived from Clark Field. Brereton directed Eubank to prepare his B-17s for the raid.

At 0715hrs Brereton returned to Army Headquarters, seeking permission to attack Formosa. Sutherland again told him to stand by. Shortly after, he received a transoceanic phone call from Washington, D.C. It was General Henry "Hap" Arnold, the Army Air Force commander. Arnold informed Brereton what happened in Hawaii, to caution Brereton against getting the Philippine aircraft caught on the ground. At 0800hrs Brereton ordered the B-17s into the air, without bombs, to get them out of Clark Field before Japanese aircraft arrived. Aircraft pilots were told to "patrol."

At 1000hrs Brereton again called Sutherland, requesting permission to attack. Again, Sutherland denied the request. Since Sutherland had not denied permission for photoreconnaissance flights, Brereton directed Eubank to conduct a photoreconnaissance flight over southern Formosa. Almost immediately after the reconnaissance flight began Brereton finally heard from MacArthur. MacArthur, in

Pilots of the 20th Pursuit Squadron pose for a group picture prior to war. Stationed at Clark Field, this squadron scrambled at 0800hrs and spent the early morning patrolling near Rosales. They were refueling at Clark Field when the Japanese attacked. (NMAF)

consultation with Brereton, agreed to permit an attack Formosa that afternoon, once the photoreconnaissance aircraft returned.

At 1120hrs, Brereton sent operational orders to Clark Field authorizing a two-squadron B-17 strike on Formosa that afternoon. Plans were set in train to have the two B-17 squadrons at Del Monte shuttle to Luzon, refuel at San Marcelino, and join the afternoon attack on Formosa. By 1130hrs the B-17s were back on the ground being fueled and loaded with 100lb and 300lb bombs for the afternoon Formosa raid. The bombers were not dispersed, but close together to simplify servicing them. Four were lined up wingtip-to-wingtip on their hardstands.

Then the P-40s from Clark and Nichols Fields landed. They had been up all morning hunting, but not finding, Japanese planes. The fighters needed fuel. Ground crews fueled and serviced them. It was also close to lunchtime. The pilots from the Clark Field squadron went to the mess hall to eat, where they joined the bomber crews already there.

The US fighters had spent a busy morning. At 0800hrs the 20th Pursuit Squadron at Clark Field was ordered aloft and told to cover Rosales, ten miles south and east of Lingayen Gulf. To cover Clark Field, the two fighter squadrons at Nichols Field, the 17th and 21st, were sent, departing at 0800hrs. Told a large formation of Japanese bombers heading towards Clark Field had been detected around 0900hrs, they set up a patrol line near Tarlac, a town north of Clark Field, flying in a long oval east and west. Fighter squadrons at Del Carmen and Iba were alerted at 0800hrs, but kept on the ground in reserve, fueled and armed with pilots in the cockpits.

There were only two Japanese raids by that part of the morning. Conditions cleared enough to permit two small Imperial Army formations to attack the barracks at Baguio and the airfield at Tuguegarao. Ki-21s were sent to Baguio, while Ki-48 bombers hit Tuguegarao, 43 in all. Both cities are in northern Luzon, north of Lingayen Gulf. The Baguio force flew down Lingayen Bay before turning east and then north to attack Baguio. This was the force US radar thought heading to Clark Field. The fighters over Rosales spotted the Japanese, which turned away before the P-40s could intercept them.

## Attack on Clark Field, December 8, 1941

Fogged in at their Formosan airfields, the Imperial Army's air force was unable to launch its first strike against the main US airfield, Clark Field, at daybreak as planned. Instead, they attacked at noon, with stunning results. What the Japanese considered a misfortune in the predawn hours proved to be the biggest gift fate could grant them that noon. The aircraft of the Far East Air Force had scrambled in the morning when word of Pearl Harbor reached them anticipating a morning attack, which never came. Had the Japanese attacked as planned they would have found an empty airfield.

By noon the US aircraft were on the ground again, refueling as their crews ate lunch. By then, a feeling of complacency had set in, left wondering where the Japanese were or even if they were really at war. Many reverted to peacetime practices. To simplify service and refueling, five B-17s were parked wingtip-to-wingtip, minimizing the distance ground crews needed to move.

The Japanese caught Clark Field napping. The resulting attack was crippling. The Japanese bombers hit the runways, catching a fighter squadron as it was taking off for its midday patrol. Only three got airborne, where a swarm of over 50 Mitsubishi Zeros met them. The bombers next hit buildings, hangars, workshops, and barracks before moving onto aircraft on the ground.

After the bombers left, the fighters moved in. They strafed the aircraft, which were largely untouched so far. Parked aircraft are relatively poor targets for bombers over 20,000ft high. They are easy targets for strafing fighters, and fully fueled aircraft, like parked B-17s, wingtip-to-wingtip burn easily. The ground crews servicing them can only run.

This plate captures the end stage of the attack on Clark Field. Imperial Navy Zeros have driven the surviving US fighters off, and are concentrating on destroying any US aircraft they see on the ground. The raid takes an especially heavy toll on the B-17s. Of 17 B-17s on the ground at Clark Field only one escaped damage. Twelve were destroyed and four damaged.

Japan launched massive airstrikes against Clark Field and Iba Field at noon on December 8. Both attacks opened with high-altitude bombing attacks by over 50 aircraft. Among them were the Mitsubishi G3Ms of the 1st Kokutai. (AC)

At 1100hrs, the telephone and telegraph lines at Iba went dead. Further communications with Nielson Field that day had to go by radio. This delayed communications, as messages had to be enciphered before sending and deciphered upon receipt. A further delay in sending messages to and from the radio room resulted. It meant radar information gathered at Iba was out of date by the time it could be relayed to other airfields. Iba became the only airfield which could use it.

The failure proved fatal. By mid-morning the Formosa airfields had cleared. At 1015hrs, 108 G3Ms and G4Ms escorted by 84 A6M Zero fighters finally departed Formosa to attack Iba and Clark Fields. This was the 11th Kotu Kantai's first string, their most experienced and capable pilots and aircrew. It was detected incoming at 1130hrs, evaluated as heading to Clark Field. At 1145hrs Nielson Field sent an attack warning to Clark Field by teletype and radio.

It never arrived. In a cascade of failure, the teletype failed and either the radio signal was jammed or the Clark Field radio left unmonitored as the operator went for lunch. The P-35-equipped 34th Pursuit Squadron at Del Carmen, ordered to cover Clark Field while the P-40s refueled, were late. Dust on their airfield delayed take-off. Worse, the 3rd Pursuit Squadron stationed at Iba Field was returning to base after a long, fruitless search for a Japanese formation reported to the west, over the China Sea. Critically low on fuel they arrived in the midst of a Japanese attack on their field.

At 1215hrs the Clark Field fighter squadron was lining up on the runway to take off when the Japanese arrived. The Japanese had achieved total tactical surprise. Its amazed pilots were greeted by the sight of a filled enemy airfield. Coming in from 22,000–25,000ft a first wave of 27 bombers in perfect formation dropped their bombs on the airfield as Clark Field's air raid siren sounded. They targeted aircraft and buildings alike, bombing under perfect conditions. Clark was protected by several batteries of 3in guns from the 200th Antiaircraft Regiment, but their shells impotently burst below the bombers.

A second wave of 27 bombers followed. Facing no aerial opposition, and seeing the antiaircraft shells bursting under them, they loitered over the airfield. They spent 15 minutes working over Clark Field, picking out individual targets, almost as if on bombing practice. Then 34 A6M fighters swept in strafing the grounded B-17s and P-40s.They spent an additional hour attacking the field, igniting fires and detonating bomb-filled aircraft.

Three P-40s managed to get airborne and the P-35s from Del Carmen arrived during the raid. The P-35 were completely outclassed by the Zeros, but ended the fight without loss due to their sturdy build and skilled flying. The P-40s claimed to have downed three or four

Japanese aircraft, the P-35s three. Even if all the claims were accurate, it was a poor return for the damage done to Clark Field.

Simultaneously, 54 G3Ms and G4Ms accompanied by 50 A6Ms struck Iba Field. They too came in at high altitude, so high that US fighters could not intercept them. The fighters had flown without oxygen, and any altitude above 18,000ft guaranteed anoxia. By the time the raid was over, Iba was ruined. The radar was destroyed. So were barracks, warehouses, workshops, and ground support equipment. Ground crews suffered heavy casualties. The entire radar crew were killed.

The 12 airborne P-40s of the squadron there arrived to refuel while the raid was occurring. They did keep the Japanese fighters engaged in air combat, so Iba was not strafed. The pilots of the 3rd were even credited with two probable kills of Zeros, but most of the P-40s were lost. By the time the raid ended, of the 18 P-40Es the squadron began the day with, only two remained.

There was a little good news. Of the two fighter squadrons from Nichols Field sent to provide air cover to Clark Field, one, the 17th, had landed at Clark Field to refuel. However, Japanese aircraft had been reported heading to Bataan or Corregidor. Skipping lunch, these pilots responded to the call departing Clark Field at 1130hrs, 15 minutes before the Japanese arrived. They were on their way to Bataan when the attack started. Once there, they spent the next few hours circling the approaches to Manila Bay. They accomplished little, but survived the day.

The 21st returned to Nichols Field to refuel and they, too, returned to the air at 1130hrs after refueling. One section of six aircraft returned to patrol over Clark Field, arriving during the raid. Three of these P-40s were lost, two to engine failure. The remaining 12 P-40s were sent to protect Cavite. As with the aircraft of the 17th, they spent the rest of the early afternoon circling, without contacting the enemy, but they, too, survived.

In all, the FEAF lost 18 of its 34 B-17s and approximately 45 P-40s, two-thirds of those in the Philippines. Iba and Clark Field had been razed. Only one early warning radar was now operational. (Since one crew was dead, the five unused sets could not be brought into service. The limitation was trained crews.) Additionally, all the US had faced to this point was the Imperial Navy. By 1300hrs the Imperial Navy was done for the day, returning to its home bases with trivial losses.

Imperial Army aircraft focused on Northern Luzon, preparing that part of the island for invasion. Its fighters were in Formosa, lacking the range to loiter over Luzon until they moved to Batan. Its bombers were attacking military targets north of 16 degrees latitude, in preparation for landings scheduled at Aparri and Vigan on December 10. They were unescorted, easy targets for any US fighters. Those were all engaged well to the south.

That evening *Langley* slipped out of Cavite, where it had been supporting the 10th Patrol Wing stationed there. Escorted by two destroyers, it steamed to Iloilo Bay, where the Asiatic Fleet ships in the Philippines were assembling. It was just the opening day of the war and the FEAF was already at half-strength. Japanese air forces were virtually untouched, and their land units were on the move.

## Tipping point – December 9–10, 1941

The next day began with a predawn raid on Nichols Field. Only seven Imperial Navy bombers hit the base (another night of fog in Formosa prevented more being sent), but they were enough. They inflicted significant damage at Nichols, destroyed another two or three P-40s, destroyed a B-18, and damaged several other aircraft. The FEAF reduced their P-40 force still further with nighttime operations by inexperienced pilots. Two or three P-40s were lost, with one pilot killed.

## EVENTS

1. 1145hrs. Iba radar detects incoming Japanese air raid determined to be heading towards Clark Field. Word fails to reach Clark Field.
2. 1215hrs. Takao Kokutai Kantai 1 bombs Clark Field.
3. 1216hrs. Three 3rd Pursuit Squadron P-40s take off from Clark Field as it is attacked. They engage Japanese fighters.
4. 1230hrs. 34th Pursuit Squadron P-35s take off from Del Carmen.
5. 1240hrs. Takao Kokutai Kantai 1 departs.
6. 1240hrs. 34th Pursuit Squadron arrives at Clark Field and engages Japanese fighters.
7. 1245hrs. Takao Kokutai Kantai 2 bombs Clark Field.
8. 1300–1330hrs. Tainan Kokutai A6Ms strafe Clark Field after chasing off US fighter aircraft.
9. 1300hrs. Takao Kokutai Kantai 2 departs.
10. 1350hrs. Surviving US fighters return to base.

# Massacre at Clark Field

At 1245hrs on December 8, 1941, 54 Japanese bombers and an equal number of fighters from the Tainan and Takao Kokutai attacked Clark Field, the main airfield of the US FEAF. Despite occurring nearly ten hours after Japan's attack at Pearl Harbor, the attack caught the US by surprise, its aircraft on the ground. Over the next hour, 30 P-40s and 12 B-17s were destroyed, another five B-17s damaged.

Patrol Wing 10 finally found a target on December 10. After a freighter fired at a snooping PBY, strike PBYs bombed it. It proved a friendly fire incident. The ship, Norwegian-flagged *Ulysses*, thought the PBYs were Japanese flying boats. The PBYs interpreted the fire as coming from a Japanese freighter. (USNHHC)

At 0730hrs the first US counterstrike began. Six B-17s, armed with 2,000lbs of 100lb bombs, took off from Del Monte to reconnoiter Catanduanes, an island east of Legaspi. Reports of Japanese activity in that area had been received, but when the bombers arrived, they found nothing. Flying on to Clark Field, they landed, refueled, and took off again, remaining airborne until dark, to avoid getting trapped on the ground.

Clark Field ground crews pieced together two flyable B-17s from B-17s damaged on December 8, leaving three B-17s there. One left Clark Field at 0800hrs on a photoreconnaissance mission to Formosa. The only aircraft available for reconnaissance, it turned back at Luzon's northern coast due to generator problems. No other B-17s were equipped with photographic equipment so the mission was cancelled.

To improve antiaircraft defenses, a battery of 3in guns from the 60th Coastal Artillery (AA) was shifted from Corregidor to Manila that day, where they could cover Nichols Field and oil storage and railyards near Nichols. The 200th Coastal Artillery (AA) sent 500 men to Manila, where, equipping from guns at the Philippine Ordnance Depot, they formed a provisional antiaircraft regiment, the 515th Coastal Artillery (AA). The guns were distributed around Manila.

Patrol Wing 10 continued patrolling the South China Sea west and northwest of Luzon. The only contacts made proved friendly fire. Spotting a lone freighter west of Luzon, a patrolling PBY closed to investigate. It was fired upon. The pilot broke away, the waist gunner returned fire. Three bomb-armed strike PBYs were called in, and attacked the "Japanese" freighter. All 12 500lb bombs dropped missed. Fortunately, neither side suffered damage or casualties. The ship was the Norwegian freighter *Ulysses*. The next morning's *Manila Bulletin* ran adjacent headlines: "PBYS BOMB JAP SHIP" and "FREIGHTER REPELS JAP BOMBERS." Less fortunate was a PBY landing at Subic Bay. It was shot up by a trigger-happy antiaircraft battery. The PBY was damaged and two crewmen badly injured.

At 1430hrs six B-17s took off from Del Monte for Luzon. They flew to San Marcelino, an auxiliary field, and landed after dark. No food was available, and the crews slept in their planes that night. Planned was a combined strike by all available B-17s, nine at Clark and six at San Marcelino the next morning. As at Subic, there was friendly fire; antiaircraft gunners fired on one B-17 as it landed.

The 14th Army opened December 10 with landings at Aparri (shown) and Vigan, in Northern Luzon. The objective for both landings was to secure airfields near the towns so Imperial Army aircraft could provide air cover for the main Lingayen Bay landings. (NARA)

Except for the bombers attacking Nichols, the Imperial Navy Air Service was largely inactive on December 9. Bad weather over Formosa, especially over western Formosa, kept them grounded. Imperial Army aircraft were more active. Ki-27s of the 50th Sentai flew to Batan Island from Formosa, to better support the next day's Vigan and Aparri landings. Bombers kept up pressure on Northern Luzon, flying missions to isolate the landing beaches.

In the pre-dawn hours of December 10, convoys carrying the Kanno Detachment landing at Vigan and the Tanaka Detachment to Aparri arrived, anchoring off the invasion beaches. The convoys had been at sea since December 7, with fighters from the 24th and 50th Sentai providing air cover during daylight hours. The convoys passed undetected by US aircraft. Patrol Wing 10 had searched the seas west of their course, while Army B-17s had held back as a strike force, rather than being used to patrol the straits between Formosa and Luzon.

Each convoy was escorted by a destroyer division, six or seven destroyers led by a light cruiser. A force of two heavy and one light cruisers, two destroyers and a seaplane tender covered the invasion convoys.

At 0550hrs, as civil twilight broke, landing operations began. Rough seas at both beaches frustrated landing plans. At Aparri two companies landed before the commander abandoned the effort. The rest of the Tanaka Detachment came ashore at Gonzaga in the lee of Cape Engano, 20 miles east of Aparri, an hour later than scheduled. At Vigan, rough seas permitted only a small number of the Kanno detachment to come ashore at Pandan, the intended landing beach. The rest remained aboard transports until the troops which landed took Vigan at 1030hrs. At daylight Ki-27s from 50th Sentai provided air cover for the Tanaka Force convoy while those of the 24th Sentai protected the Kanno Detachment convoy. Aparri was defended by an untrained, half-strength company of the Philippine 12th Infantry Regiment. Vigan was undefended.

The delays provided an opportunity for the FEAF to smash the invasions. The landings at Aparri were reported by the commander of the Philippine company stationed there shortly after the Japanese landed. Badly outnumbered by even the two Japanese companies landed, it withdrew south. A P-40 flying reconnaissance spotted the Vigan convoy at 0513hrs and

## **OPPOSITE** AIR ACTIVITY, DECEMBER 10, 1941

The US counterattacked the invasions with B-17 raids against both beachheads. The damage done by the B-17s was slight, almost trivial. They sank a small minesweeper, and possibly a transport, and slightly damaged several other ships. It did not stop the landings. (NMAF)

called in the sighting. Alerted by one of its own aircraft, the FEAF reacted to the Vigan landing first.

Six B-17s at Clark Field were available, readied for morning strike missions in the predawn hours. At 0530hrs one was pulled from the strike force to conduct aerial photoreconnaissance of Formosa. At 0600hrs the remaining five B-17s, escorted by six P-40s took off for Vigan. Sixteen P-35s, from Del Carmen, armed with 100lb bombs, joined the attack.

The B-17s arrived first, making individual attacks. Each carried 20 100lb demolition bombs. They picked out anchored, unloading transports as targets. Two B-17s attacked at 12,000ft, two others at 12,500ft. Each plane made two passes, dropping half their bombs on each run. The fifth B-17 attacked at 10,000ft on its first pass and 7,000ft on the second. The bombs caused only minor damage, through near-misses.

The P-40s came in next, strafing the landing barges and Japanese already ashore. Finally, the slow, unarmored P-35s arrived. Only seven reached Vigan. The rest turned back due to engine trouble or bad weather. They made low passes, strafing and dropping their bombs. Three transports were hit, and several landing barges beached to keep them from sinking. One P-35, flown by the squadron commander, went down, caught in the explosion when the ship he was attacking blew up. The explosion may have been due to his bomb or earlier damage caused by a B-17. A second P-35 had engine trouble over Vigan; its pilot bailed out. The other five P-35s made it back to Del Carmen, where the eight planes that had turned back were already waiting.

There was no opposition by the 24th Sentai. The attack had been made during a gap in air coverage. Since a fighter sentai had at most 36 aircraft, only a few could be in the air at one time and coverage gaps were inevitable. The returning US pilots reported "fierce" antiaircraft fire, but this judgement was due more to inexperience than reality. There were only 13 ships off Vigan: six destroyers, six transports and a light cruiser. None had a formidable suite of antiaircraft guns. The cruiser had two 76mm antiaircraft guns and two machine guns. The rest carried only light antiaircraft guns.

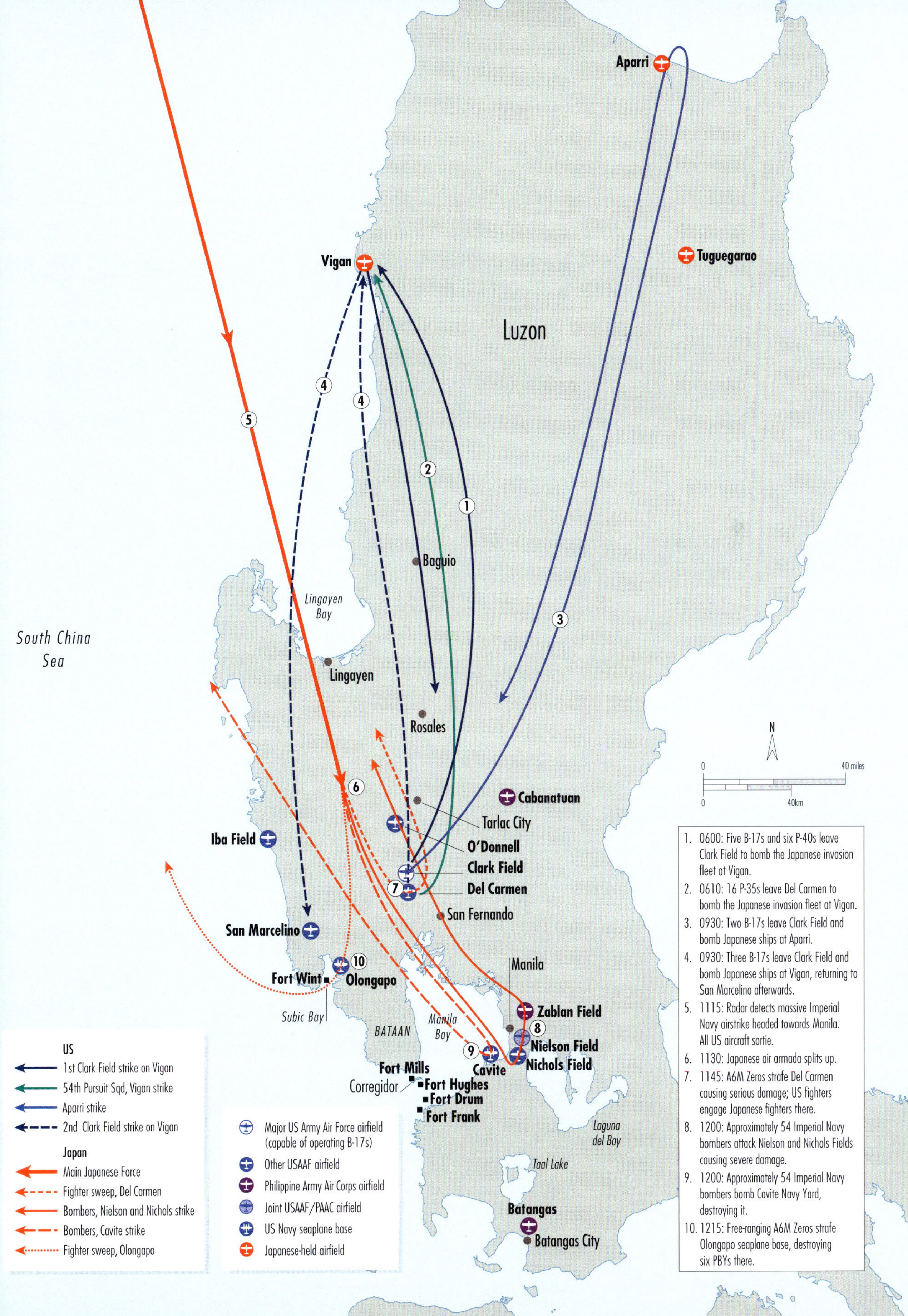
Aparri
Tuguegarao
Vigan
Luzon
Baguio
Lingayen Bay
South China Sea
Lingayen
Rosales
Cabanatuan
Tarlac City
O'Donnell
Clark Field
Del Carmen
San Fernando
Iba Field
San Marcelino
Fort Wint
Olongapo
Subic Bay
BATAAN
Manila
Manila Bay
Zablan Field
Nielson Field
Nichols Field
Cavite
Fort Mills
Corregidor
Fort Hughes
Fort Drum
Fort Frank
Laguna del Bay
Taal Lake
Batangas
Batangas City
N
0
40 miles
0
40km
US
1st Clark Field strike on Vigan
54th Pursuit Sqd, Vigan strike
Aparri strike
2nd Clark Field strike on Vigan
Japan
Main Japanese Force
Fighter sweep, Del Carmen
Bombers, Nielson and Nichols strike
Bombers, Cavite strike
Fighter sweep, Olongapo
Major US Army Air Force airfield (capable of operating B-17s)
Other USAAF airfield
Philippine Army Air Corps airfield
Joint USAAF/PAAC airfield
US Navy seaplane base
Japanese-held airfield
1. 0600: Five B-17s and six P-40s leave Clark Field to bomb the Japanese invasion fleet at Vigan.
2. 0610: 16 P-35s leave Del Carmen to bomb the Japanese invasion fleet at Vigan.
3. 0930: Two B-17s leave Clark Field and bomb Japanese ships at Aparri.
4. 0930: Three B-17s leave Clark Field and bomb Japanese ships at Vigan, returning to San Marcelino afterwards.
5. 1115: Radar detects massive Imperial Navy airstrike headed towards Manila. All US aircraft sortie.
6. 1130: Japanese air armada splits up.
7. 1145: A6M Zeros strafe Del Carmen causing serious damage; US fighters engage Japanese fighters there.
8. 1200: Approximately 54 Imperial Navy bombers attack Nielson and Nichols Fields causing severe damage.
9. 1200: Approximately 54 Imperial Navy bombers bomb Cavite Navy Yard, destroying it.
10. 1215: Free-ranging A6M Zeros strafe Olongapo seaplane base, destroying six PBYs there.

On December 10, Japanese aircraft visited airfields they had neglected on the first two days of battle. While Nielson and Nichols Fields were the main targets, marauding Zeros strafed Del Carmen in advance of the other raids. They caught most of the 34th Pursuit Squadron's P-35s on the ground and destroyed them. (AC)

The US attack on the Aparri landing occurred later, with fewer aircraft. Five B-17s from San Marcelino flew to Clark Field to refuel and arm. Two left Clark Field at 0930hrs. Their primary target was an aircraft carrier erroneously reported to be with the convoy. The first, armed with eight 600lb demolition bombs, seeing no aircraft carrier, spread his bombs among the transports. He reported one hit.

The second plane, flown by Captain Colin Kelly had only three 600lb bombs aboard. Not seeing a carrier, he targeted what he identified as a Fuso-class battleship. It was really the light cruiser *Natori*. Japan's nearest battleship was off Malaya. He made three runs on the target dropping his bombs on it, scoring only near-misses, and slightly damaging the cruiser and a nearby destroyer. The after-action report got improved upward. The Fuso-class battleship became the battlecruiser *Haruna* and one reported hit became the battleship was sunk.

Ki-27s of the 50th Sentai were present when the bombers attacked. They intercepted the first B-17, but only after it dropped its bombs. That B-17 received only minor damage and outran the Ki-27. Kelly's aircraft was too high, at 20,000ft, for successful interception. While returning to Clark Field, Kelly was spotted and intercepted by A6Ms of the Tainan Kokutai, conducting a pre-strike sweep prior to an attack at Clark Field. They shot Kelly's plane down. He died allowing the other crewmembers to escape. All but one survived bailout. The dead Kelly gave the US its first hero of the war.

The three other B-17s struck the Vigan beachhead. One, commanded by Major Emmett O'Donnell, dropped eight 600lb bombs on transports and observed no hits. The second made two runs at 12,500ft, dropping seven 300lb demolition bombs. It missed the targeted destroyers on the first pass, but observed one hit on a transport on the second. The third, armed with a single 600lb bomb, dropped at 25,000ft and claimed a hit on a transport.

This time all three B-17s ran into fighter opposition. While unable to prevent the bombers from attacking, they got their revenge on the way out. One bomber was severely damaged, but managed to escape without casualties, reaching San Marcelino safely.

This marked the end of US air activities against the landing forces that day. Air raid warnings at Clark Field made it inadvisable for the bombers to return. Instead, they were

Cavite Navy Yard was another major target on December 10. Virtually everything of value was destroyed: fuel storage, warehouses, machine shops, and docks. The only thing missed were the ammunition magazines. Its contents were transferred to Mariveles and Corregidor the next day, as Cavite was abandoned. (AC)

hastily refueled and ordered back to Del Monte. Because they had not been fully fueled, one landed at Tacloban on Leyte and two at San Jose, Mindoro, to refuel.

The reward for the attacks was paltry. The minesweeper *W-10* was bombed and sunk by a P-35 at Vigan. B-17s damaged the light cruiser *Naka* and transport *Takao Maru* (which was beached). Strafing damaged the destroyer *Murasame* and transport *Oigawa Maru*. At Aparri, the minesweeper *W-19* was destroyed, in addition to the two ships Kelly damaged. That was it.

## Colin Kelly attacks the IJN *Natori*, December 10, 1941

On December 10, following confirmation of reports the Japanese were landing troops at Aparri, two B-17s were sent to attack the invasion fleet. A Japanese aircraft carrier was reportedly there, and the B-17s were told it was their primary target. One B-17 was flown by Colin Kelly, a Regular Army officer who arrived with the first batch of B-17s sent to the Far East.

His bomber was sent off before it could be fully fueled or fully armed ahead of flying to Aparri. There was time to load only three 600lb bombs before an air raid warning forced a premature departure from Clark Field. Under-armed and under-briefed, Kelly set out for Aparri.

When he got there, he and his crew spotted ships off the coast. One was much larger than the others. It was the light cruiser *Natori*, at 5,100 tons it was twice the size of the destroyers, minesweepers, and patrol craft it accompanied. They assumed it was a battleship, identifying it as Fuso-class. Since Fusos had six centerline turrets and two funnels, *Natori* with five centerline turrets and three funnels sort of resembled *Fuso*. Especially as from 20,000ft up it was easy to confuse the third funnel for a turret.

It was not the carrier they were sent after. Initially Kelly ignored it, searching further for the aircraft carrier. Unable to find it (there was no carrier to be found) Kelly decided a battleship made an adequate consolation prize. They turned back, found it, and made three passes on it at 20,000ft.

The first two passes were practice runs, allowing the bombardier to fine-tune his bombsight. On the third pass, the bombardier dropped his three demolition bombs. It was as perfect a drop as a bombardier could wish for. The three bombs bracketed *Natori*, slightly damaging it and an accompanying destroyer. From 20,000ft the nearest near-miss appeared to be a direct hit, and was reported as such.

This plate shows *Natori* as the bombs splashed around it.

By 1300hrs the Japanese occupied both towns' airfields, and airfield units began readying them for Japanese aircraft. By nightfall, the first Imperial Army Sentai began arriving. Japan had working airfields on Luzon, simplifying the task of providing air support to Japanese troops.

The first warning of the Japanese attack came at 1115hrs from the remaining radar station at Manila. This gave 45 minutes warning. Observations indicated the Manila area was the target, and Interceptor Command at Nielson sent up everything available: 20 P-40s, 15 P-35s, and perhaps two PAAC P-26s. At Clark Field everything flyable took off, including B-17s only partially armed and fueled.

The Japanese air armada split north of Manila Bay, with half heading towards Manila and the other half pushing south for Cavite. Del Carmen, home to the 34th Pursuit Squadron of P-35s, was hit first, about 30 minutes after the alert was first raised. A6M Zeros strafed the base, destroying any aircraft then on the ground, and heavily damaging any buildings. US fighters caught the Japanese there, and shot down four.

This pulled US aircraft from the main Nichols and Nielson attacks. Fifty-four bombers attacked the airfield, making level passes at altitudes above the reach of antiaircraft guns. The bomb runs were slow and deliberate. The escorting Zeros kept what few US fighters were in the air there from reaching the bombers. The US P-40s ended up in dozens of individual dogfights with the escorting Zeros at altitudes below 5,000ft. Damage to Nichols was compounded because the previous shift of P-40s flying combat patrol had just landed and were being serviced as the attack began. Once the Japanese decided Nichols had enough damage, the remaining armed bombers shifted to nearby Nielson Field, two miles away.

Concurrent with the US Army airfields attacks, Cavite was also getting worked over. Fifty-four G3Ms and G4Ms accompanied by 50 A6Ms attacked just after 1200hrs. As elsewhere, the bombers remained high, too high for antiaircraft fire, while the fighters swept in low, strafing. Half the bombers hit ships in Cavite Bay, the other half attacked shore facilities. They flew above the maximum altitude of the antiaircraft guns at Cavite, allowing straight and deliberate bomb runs.

Cavite was obliterated. The power plant, workshops, industrial facilities, and supply depots were ruined. Fires started that noon raged until the next day. The submarine *Sealion*, minesweeper *Bittern*, and ferry launch *Santa Rita* were sunk or so badly damaged they were scuttled. Destroyers *Peary* (DD-226) and *Pillsbury* (DD-227), submarine *Seadragon*, and submarine tender *Otus* were damaged.

The PBYs of Patrol Wing 10 had discovered a Japanese naval force in the South China Sea, possibly one moving south to the Dutch East Indies, that morning. After attacking it, they returned to Cavite to refuel and rearm. They were taking off when the attack began. A swarm of A6Ms swept over the seaplane base shooting it up before pushing on to Cavite. Three PBYs were destroyed. A fourth was damaged, but managed to shoot down a Zero, the US Navy's first aerial kill of World War II.

Admiral Hart watched the attack from his office in his headquarters at Manila's Marsman Building, near Manila's commercial harbor. That night he sent all US Navy ships capable of putting to sea out of Cavite and ordered vessels incapable of movement scuttled. Only the submarine tender *Canopus*, four small minesweepers, six PT boats, and three river gunboats brought to the Philippines from China remained in the Philippines, operating out of Corregidor and the Bataan harbor of Mariveles.

## Retreat – December 11–14, 1941

As the sun rose on December 11, the air campaign had slipped irrevocably in Japan's favor. Japan held two airfields on Luzon. The 5th Hikoshidan was moving fighters and

By December 11 Imperial Army warplanes were operating out of airfields on Luzon. That allowed the short-ranged Ki-27s to provide air cover for Japanese forces on Luzon and its light bombers to quickly provide ground support to advancing Japanese troops. (NARA)

single-engine bombers from the 16th Sentai, with its Ki-30 attack aircraft, to them, extending its air umbrella over northern Luzon. US ground forces in the immediate area, the 11th Philippine Division, were understrength, undertrained, underequipped, and widely scattered.

The US had lost most of its air force. By the close of December 10, it had 22 surviving P-40s and eight P-35s. Six more damaged P-40s, three each at Nichols and Clark Fields were being repaired and expected to be back in service by December 12. There were 16 B-17s left, only seven undamaged. Five others could be used for low-level missions, and four others were out of service pending repairs. All trainers, observation airplanes, and attack aircraft were destroyed. A few B-18s survived. The PAAC still had two B-10s and its fighter squadron available, but the fighters were obsolete P-26s. Patrol Wing 10 had lost one-third of its aircraft.

Owing to losses, Brereton instituted two changes in policy. Surviving aircraft were to be husbanded to be available when the main Japanese landings occurred – the US recognized the previous day's landings were intended to secure airfields to provide air cover for the main landing. Further, aerial reconnaissance was badly needed. Only the P-40s could conduct it in the face of Japanese air superiority.

The FEAF opted to stop intercepting Japanese air raids. Instead, fighters would go up individually as scouts. If worthwhile targets were found, the surviving B-17s would attack them, escorted by fighters. The fighter pilots resented this new policy, feeling they would be denied a chance to attack the enemy. They were permitted to defend themselves, and many pilots used the concept of "defense" elastically, given any opportunity.

December 11 would prove a relatively quiet day in the air. By the time the Imperial Navy's aircraft were returning from the previous day's strikes at Manila and Cavite, weather over Formosa was so bad that returning aircraft had to land at any available airfield. Units were scattered and mixed throughout southern Formosa. Since weather continued to be bad on December 11, the Imperial Navy cancelled most planned strikes against the remaining US aviation and military infrastructure south of the 16th parallel. It conducted a few small missions against US airfields in Luzon.

The landing at Legaspi was done for the same reason as the ones at Aparri and Vigan: to secure an airfield from which Japanese aircraft could provide air cover for a later, main landing. The airfield at Legaspi was small, but Japanese fighters could operate from it. (NARA)

The Imperial Army spent the day consolidating its position in northern Luzon, improving the airfields they had taken, moving air units into them, and expanding their beachhead. Its ground troops pushed down the Cagayan River, taking Tuguegarao, and its airfield. The Imperial Japanese Army Air Service (IJAAS) began using it the next day.

The US Navy spent the day abandoning Cavite. Surprisingly, the ammunition depot was untouched. Its contents were moved to Corregidor and Mariveles, as were all remaining ships. Surviving stores were also moved and camouflaged. The only unit to remain at Cavite was the ground crew for the Sangley Point seaplane base. Patrol Wing 10 aircraft normally operating there were moved to nearby anchorages, typically at Laguna del Bay, immediately southeast of Cavite. They returned only to refuel, arm, and receive maintenance.

The FEAF used the day to catch its breath and reorganize. Aircraft were hastily repaired. At airfields, rubble was cleared, and what repairs could be made to buildings was done. The B-17s, scattered all over the central Philippines as December 10 ended, were flown to Del Monte, their new home base. Luzon airfields would be used for refueling to stage missions to Formosa (there were still hopes of striking there), but the Fortresses were to return to Del Monte at the end of the day.

Arnold, in Washington, had learned of the disaster in the Philippines, especially that aircraft were caught on the ground and destroyed at Clark and Iba Fields. He was convinced there had to be a mistake. One of the few things working in the Philippines were long-distance phone lines and, on December 11, Brereton received a second transoceanic phone call from Washington, D.C. In it, Arnold wanted to know "what the hell had happened?" Especially after Arnold had talked to Brereton earlier, warning Brereton not to get caught with his planes on the ground.

Any explanation Brereton gave sounded like an excuse to Arnold. Perhaps fortunately for Brereton, the Imperial Navy made one of its few attacks of the day during the phone call, strafing Nielson Field. Hearing commotion, Arnold demanded, "What in the hell is going on there?" "We are having visitors," Brereton replied, ending the call.

The attack on Nielson Field typified Imperial Navy attacks throughout that day – small nuisance raids. A lone G3M attacked the PBYs at Laguna del Bay, destroying one engine on one PBY. Similar attacks kept US forces on edge the rest of the day.

December 12 followed the pattern set on December 8 and 10. The Imperial Navy launched a massive set of airstrikes, totaling over 100 bombers on airfields south of 16 degrees North. It was also the day the Japanese launched their third preparatory invasion, this one at Legaspi near Luzon's southern end.

Captain Jesus Villamor in the cockpit of his P-26. He commanded the PAAC 6th Pursuit Squadron. In a wild melee with Japanese Zeros, Villamor claimed two kills. He shot down three Japanese aircraft in December 1941: two G3Ms and a Zero. (LOC)

The day opened with the Kimura Detachment landing at Legaspi. A regiment-sized unit with an Imperial Navy airfield construction unit attached, it landed at dawn. The invasion was covered by the light carrier *Ryujo*, which attacked Davao four days earlier. Its aircraft provided air cover, which proved unnecessary initially, since there were no defenders. As with the northern landings, securing an airfield was this landing's goal. The nearest US forces were 150 miles away. The airfield was in Japanese hands by 0900hrs. The southern terminus of the Manila railroad fell soon after, but not before the stationmaster called Manila to report the seizure.

Two US fighters were sent to investigate shortly after the stationmaster's report. They found the airfield occupied and strafed it. No follow-up was possible that day as the Japanese renewed their attacks on US airfields. All the US could do was evacuate rolling stock, prepare the railroad bridges for demolition, and send two companies of the Philippine 51st division to block the approach route to Manila. The airfield was open for operation that evening.

Imperial Army aircraft made their first appearance over central Luzon that day. Its bombers struck Del Carmen, Clark Field, Baguio in the hills east of Lingayen Bay, and Tarlac in the

## Battle of Batangas Field, December 12, 1941

Captain Jesus A. Villamor commanded the PAAC's only fighter squadron in December 1941. It flew P-26s, an aircraft that was the hottest fighter of its day. But its day was 1932, and by 1941 it was obsolete. It could possibly hold its own against the Ki-27, but was completely outclassed by the A6M Zero. That mattered little to Villamor and the pilots of his squadron.

By December 12 he had faced the Japanese already, having fought them over Zablan on December 10. There he managed to shoot down a Zero. Then his base received word the Japanese were attacking. He took to the air with five other pilots. Once aloft he spotted a formation of 27 G3M Nells, headed towards home airfield, Batangas. They were accompanied by a formation of Zeros. Despite the odds, Villamor led his men against the Japanese.

A wild aerial melee followed. Villamor opened by making a head-on pass against the enemy bombers. To his amazement, he set one on fire. It fell out of formation, smoking, disintegrating in mid-air before reaching the ground. As he was completing this attack he and his men were swarmed by the escorting Zeros, diving out of the sun. Villamor and his wingman, Lt Cesar Basa, found themselves being attacked by four Zeros.

The only thing that saved the Filipino pair was the superior maneuverability of the slower, yet more agile Peashooter. They managed to evade the initial attack by the Zeros by a tight, climbing turn where the Zeros zoomed past without landing a hit. Their luck did not hold long. Basa and two other Peashooter pilots were shot down. Villamor and the other two P-26 pilots evaded the Zeros and landed safely at other fields. Batangas was too badly damaged to use.

This plate shows the battle at its height with Villamor and Basa fighting four Zeros, immediately after the initial attack on the bombers.

The only fighter opposition the US faced over Aparri was from the fixed-landing gear Ki-27. It was an aircraft the P-40 was clearly superior to. In single combat the P-40 generally won, but there were too few P-40s and too many Ki-27s for the US to challenge Japanese air superiority over Aparri by December 12. (AC)

Luzon Plain. The Baguio and Tarlac airstrikes hit Army targets rather than airfields. They opened the campaign to reduce US ground forces prior to the main invasion.

The Imperial Navy aircraft arrived at the Philippines mid-day. Between 1130hrs and 1200hrs 62 bombers hit Iba and Clark Fields. The main blow fell on Iba, where ten planes were destroyed on the ground. Clark had a few buildings hit. In addition to bombs, the G3Ms and G4Ms dropped leaflets. Aimed at the Filipinos, the leaflets encouraged them to support the Japanese and shun the Americans.

Another 40 bombers escorted by fighters headed towards the Manila-area airfields. These were clouded over. The Imperial Navy turned its attention elsewhere, hitting Olongapo, Del Carmen, Cabanatuan, and Batangas at least once during the day. Several were hit twice.

Freed from escort duties, one set of A6Ms swept over Olongapo. The PBYs left earlier that morning seeking a Japanese convoy reported off Luzon's western coast. The search was fruitless, and by noon had returned. They had finished refueling when the Zeros arrived. All seven PBYs were destroyed, reducing Patrol Wing 10 to half strength. Return fire from the PBYs failed to down any enemy aircraft.

Another set of A6Ms accompanied twin-engine bombers attacking Batangas. This was a PAAC base, home to their 6th Pursuit Squadron, outfitted with P-26 Peashooters. Its commander, Captain Jesus Villamor had faced the Japanese two days earlier, over Manila. Miraculously he managed to shoot down one Zero then, more through luck than skill. Now, two days later at his home base, 27 G4Ms were attacking. Six P-26s were serviceable. He led the flight up, against them.

A wild melee ensued. Villamor managed to down a G3M before being intercepted by the Zeros. In the resulting series of dogfights, four P-26s were shot down, but one of the flight's P-26s managed to down a Zero. The two surviving Peashooters landed at Zablan Field, another PAAC base. The Japanese flattened Batangas. The surviving aircraft of the 6th relocated to a temporary field at Kamuning.

The only offensive action taken by the FEAF on December 12 was an attack by two B-17s against the Vigan beachhead. One failed to get airborne after it blew a tire, the second reached Vigan and bombed the transports. No hits were obtained.

Reconnaissance flights were flown to Vigan and Aparri, and one to Legaspi. All showed depressing progress by the Japanese invasion forces. The US flew other numerous reconnaissance missions with P-40s on December 12, 13, and 14. During one flight to Aparri on December 13, the pilot, Boyd "Buzz" Wagner, encountered Ki-27s. Flying the clearly superior P-40, Boyd shot down two. For good measure he then strafed the Aparri airfield.

The previous day's pattern was repeated on December 13. The Imperial Navy set all available bombers against airfields in Luzon. Over 100, escorted by nearly as many A6M fighters, struck Iba, Clark, Del Carmen, and Nichols Fields. Over Clark Field the Imperial Army joined in, sending 15 Ki-21 heavy bombers, a first.

Batan's airfield, taken less than a week earlier, was emptied of aircraft. The fighters stationed there shifted to Aparri, Vigan, and Tuguegarao. The airfields there, on Northern Luzon, were closer to the action and so less fuel and time were exhausted when missions started from them. Batan was relegated to an emergency field for aircraft flying between Formosa and Luzon.

On December 14, the 5th Bombardment Group launched what would prove to be the B-17s' last solely Philippine-based major airstrike of the campaign. They were sent against Legaspi, in an attempt to counter the invasion there. Of the 16 B-17s at Del Monte, only six were flyable. They were armed, fueled, and sent off at 1130hrs.

Six immediately became five. The lead B-17 blew a tire on the runway, and could not get airborne. Shortly after take-off, over Camiguin Island, the formation leader experienced engine trouble. It was forced to return to Del Monte. As the formation reached Bohol a second B-17 had engine trouble. It, too, had to return to base. The three remaining B-17s continued in formation. Near the halfway point they ran into thick cloud cover and the three bombers soon lost sight of each other. They pressed on to Legaspi individually.

The first two arrived at Legaspi 90 seconds apart. Both were at 21,000ft. The first B-17 over the target, flown by Lt Jack Adams made one pass, dropping all his bombs on the ships off Legaspi. However, the Japanese had already ferried fighters to the airfield there and Adams was intercepted by six A6Ms. Upon completing the run, he dove for a cloud bank at 10,000ft. Before reaching it, the Zeros caught up and attacked. Soon two engines were dead on one wing and four crewmen injured. Adams made a crash landing on a flooded rice paddy at Masbate. The crew had just exited when one Japanese fighter spotted the wreck and strafed it. Four crewmen were injured during the attack, one fatally. The bomber was destroyed.

The second B-17, flown by Lt Eliott Vandevanter, found skies empty of enemy fighters. He made three passes over the target, dropping all his bombs. Once finished he headed into the clouds, returning to Del Monte, hidden by the weather on the first part of the return trip. He landed safely.

When the B-17s hit the weather front while heading to Legaspi, the combination of cold air and humidity caused one engine on the third B-17 to quit. The pilot, Lt Hewitt Wheless,

Ground crews load bombs into a B-17 at Del Monte Field. By December 14 all B-17 missions were being flown from Del Monte. Clark Field had been abandoned as a bomber base. This could be one of the B-17s that attacked Legaspi on December 14. (NMAF)

# The Legaspi Mission, December 14, 1941

On December 14, 1941 the 5th Bomber Command launched its final B-17 strike which began and ended in the Philippines. In response to a Japanese landing at Legaspi, it sent every flyable B-17 to bomb the troopships there, six in all. Only half the B-17s dispatched even reached Legaspi.

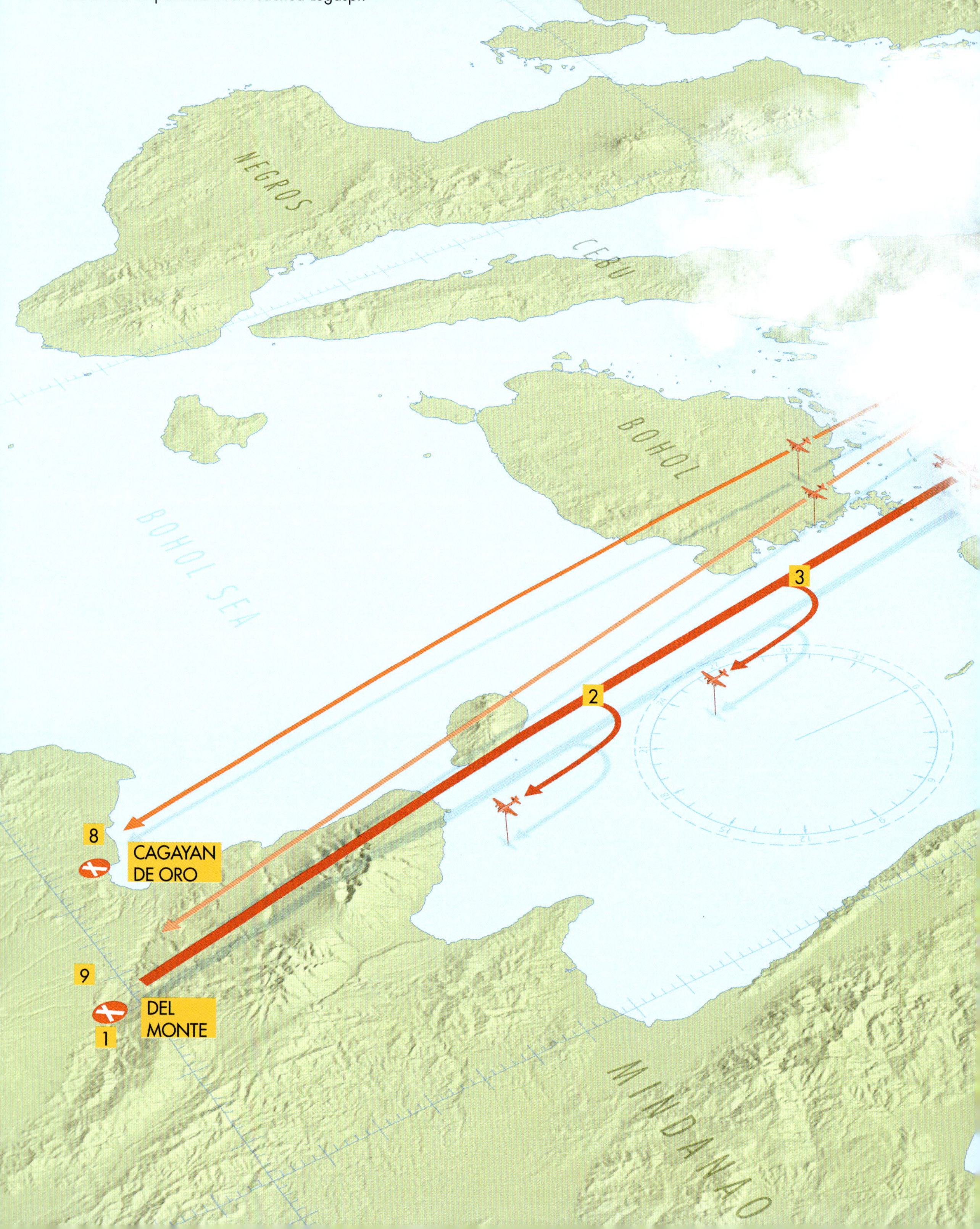

## EVENTS

1. Mission starts at Del Monte. Lt Conolly, leading the mission, has his B-17 blow a tire on take-off and fails to get airborne. Lt Coats takes command of formation.
2. Lt Coats's B-17 has engine trouble, and is forced to return to Del Monte.
3. Lt Ford's B-17 has engine trouble, and is forced to return to Del Monte.
4. Remaining aircraft run into thick clouds and lose sight of each other. They proceed independently. Lt Wheless is forced to drop to 10,000 ft due to engine icing, but continues.
5. Three B-17s arrive over target separately. Lt Adams's B-17 attacks first and is attacked by six Zeros. Lt Vandevanter attacks next with no opposition. Lt Wheless attacks last and is attacked by 18 A6Ms.
6. Lt Adams, pursued by Zeros, crash lands at Masbate. His B-17 is strafed after crew evacuated.
7. The 18 Zeros pursuing Lt Wheless turn back when they run out of ammunition. The B-17 is damaged and cannot fly above 3,000ft.
8. Lt Wheless, unable to fly over mountains to land at Del Monte, lands at Cagayan. He does not realize the runway is barricaded until too late to abort landing.
9. Lt Vandevanter lands successfully at Del Monte.

took the plane down to 10,000ft and recovered the engine. Assuming he was ahead of the other two Fortresses, he flew on, hoping to surprise the Japanese. Instead, he arrived after the other two and the Japanese were fully alerted. They were jumped by 18 fighters.

The airplane dropped its eight 600lb bombs on six transports alongside the docks at Legaspi while under attack by eight Zeros. Once the last bomb dropped, Wheless turned for home, maneuvering wildly to throw off the enemy fighters' aim. By then the Fortress was riddled with bullets, the radio operator was dead, and three gunners were wounded. The navigator and bombardier manned the guns. Enemy fighters pursued Wheless's B-17 for 30 minutes until they ran out of ammunition and broke away. The crew claimed to have shot down seven of the enemy. Postwar analysis did not bear that out.

An engine was knocked out and a gas tank so badly riddled that the fuel leaked out. The airplane arrived at Mindanao at dusk low on fuel and unable to clear the mountains between the shore and Del Monte. Wheless opted to land at Cagayan, a fighter strip on the coast. Coming in for final landing, too late to go around, he discovered the runway was barricaded and going through the barricades further damaged the bomber. The mission cost two B-17s, and came up empty. No Japanese transports were sunk; probably none were hit. Any near misses caused only minor damage.

## Withdrawal – December 15, 1941 to January 5, 1942

The war was one week old, and Japan had already achieved air superiority, something they assumed would take two weeks. As of December 15, Japanese analysts estimated US Army Air Forces strength at 20 fighters, ten bombers, and ten flying boats. They believed the US had dispersed the remaining aircraft and moved them to airfields on Iliolo, Jolo, and Mindanao.

In reality, except for the B-17s, which had moved to Del Monte in Mindanao, the US aircraft were largely still based in Luzon. Maintenance facilities in airfields outside Luzon were rudimentary, even at Del Monte. (Maintenance at Del Monte was done in open air or under tents, with spare parts flown down from Clark Field in surviving B-18s.) Surviving fighters remained at Luzon airfields, dispersed and camouflaged.

While not as impressive as high-performance aircraft, maintenance facilities like this electrical shop at Nichols Field, and the spare parts they housed, were critical to keeping warplanes flying. By the second week of war, the FEAF had lost most of its permanent facilities and was critically short of spares. (NARA)

The actual number of aircraft remaining to the USAAF were low. In some categories the US had over 50 percent more aircraft than Japan believed. In terms of flyable aircraft, the Japanese overstated US capabilities. A lack of spare parts crippled US efforts to keep planes flying. The wastage was not being caused by combat, but by accelerated wartime air operations.

Routine wear and tear required frequent replacement of tires, engine parts, and propellers. Spares were short before the war. Increased operations and destruction of warehouses at airfields had exhausted reserves. More damaged aircraft were cannibalized to keep less damaged aircraft flying. When B-17s crashed, as happened at Masbate, the crew did not burn them as doctrine required, hoping to return for salvageable parts.

Maintenance made keeping both the B-17s and PBYs based in Mindanao untenable. Japanese aircraft had not yet reached Mindanao, nor did they know the location of the B-17 field there, though Brereton realized it was only a matter of time before they did. Del Monte had no fighter cover or radar and its only antiaircraft guns were .50cal machine guns. He did not want his bombers caught on the ground again, as they had been at Clark Field. Patrol Wing 10's situation was worse – its major bases were known to the Japanese and under attack – so, on December 15, the US Army and US Navy independently decided to withdraw them.

Brereton ordered the B-17s to Batchelor Field near Darwin. From there they were to stage to Del Monte, refuel, and conduct operations in the Philippines. They could receive routine servicing at Batchelor Field, but for a full depot overhaul they could fly to Laverton near Melbourne. Between December 17 and 20, the surviving flyable B-17s at Del Monte, 14 in all, flew to Darwin. Most continued on to Laverton, for needed overhauls. Distance made mounting attacks from Australia difficult – it was nearly 1,500 miles from Batchelor Field to Del Monte – yet it offered a way to use the B-17s.

Admiral Hart ordered Patrol Wing 10's departure on December 14. At that time the 13 surviving PBYs in Luzon were at Laguna del Bay, hidden along the shoreline. Three were unflyable. Five others were at Lake Lanao in Mindanao. Nine Luzon PBYs were sent to Makassar in the Dutch East Indies on December 15, refueling at Lake Lanao. Six got the orders and left as a group. Three others never got the word and remained. That left seven PBYs near Manila, four flyable. These were temporarily held to evacuate senior and critical personnel from Manila. The rest arrived at Surabaya on December 20. The PBYs remaining in the Philippines served as air taxis between Manila and Mindanao until Manila fell.

The Japanese advanced their ground forces. By December 15, due to Japanese command of the sky and the limp response by US ground forces in northern Luzon, the Aparri and Vigan beachheads merged. The Kanno and Tanaka Detachments were combined under the command of Colonel Tanaka. They were ordered to move down the coast road from Vigan to Rosario and link up with the Main Force due to land at Lingayen Bay on December 22.

The air war over Luzon settled into a pattern over the next week. Weather permitting, Imperial Army and Imperial Navy aircraft launched daily air raids against US Army airfields and US Navy seaplane bases, Manila, and its harbor. For the Japanese, these were milk runs, unopposed by US fighters, flown above the altitude US antiaircraft could reach.

The US countered with daily reconnaissance flights by the surviving P-40s. These were interspersed with occasional attacks on Japanese-held airfields at Aparri and Vigan. On December 16 three

Lt Boyd "Buzz" Wagner shot down his fifth Japanese aircraft, a Ki-27, on December 16, 1941. He became the first US ace of World War II. He went on to shoot down three more aircraft in New Guinea before being sent home to the US. He died in a flying accident in November 1942. (NMAF)

The Japanese landed at Davao, Mindanao's largest city, on December 22. They quickly established a beachhead and captured Davao's airfield. While Del Monte was unknown to the Japanese, the beachhead put Del Monte at risk. (AC)

P-40s, with light bombs mounted, dive-bombed the Vigan airfield. One of the Warhawks was shot down. Another, flown by Wagner, shot down a Ki-27. It was Wagner's fifth kill, making him the first US ace of World War II.

The US also began constructing 17 new airfields and expanding others, using ground echelon personnel from airfields under Japanese attack. A new field was carved out of a sugar field at Lubao, just north of Manila Bay. Construction was concealed from the Japanese. Revetments were camouflaged under vegetation spread over chicken wire. The runway was disguised by rows of dead cane with the appearance of freshly harvested sugar. Two airstrips in Bataan, Bataan Airfield near the peninsula's southern tip and Orani Field at Bataan's northern end, were similarly enlarged. The Japanese missed the activity.

Nor had Washington or the FEAF abandoned reinforcing the Philippine air garrison. The A-24s and P-40s being sent to the Philippines by convoy when the war broke out were diverted to Australia and unloaded. More fighters were being shipped by sea to Australia. A fighter ferry route from Darwin to Mindanao was scouted out. Traveling through the Dutch East Indies, the fighters would make refueling stops on Timor, the Celebes, and Borneo along the way. MacArthur forcefully pushed reinforcing his air force.

Washington planned to rush 80 four-engine bombers to the Philippines. The bombers would be sent across the Atlantic and Africa to India. At Bangalore, MacArthur would take control of them. From there they would reach Mindanao by flying through the Dutch East Indies. The transfer would be complete by February 21, 1942.

Before these plans could be executed, everything fell apart. The Japanese landed the equivalent of a brigade at Davao in Mindanao on December 20. Two days later, the Japanese main landings on Luzon occurred. On December 22 elements of the 48th Infantry Division landed in Lingayen Bay. On December 24, the 16th Infantry Division landed at Lamon Bay north of Legaspi.

The Mindanao landing threatened Del Monte and Malabang (the Philippine terminus of the Australia–Philippines fighter ferry route). The primary objective of the Sakaguchi Detachment landing at Davao was Davao Airfield. It was quickly captured, giving Japanese forces an airfield within 125 miles of Del Monte. If the Japanese held Davao, enemy aircraft were only a 50-minute flight from Del Monte.

Brereton ordered a B-17 strike in an attempt to repel the invaders. On December 22, nine B-17s departed Darwin, each carrying four 500lb bombs. The 1,500-mile flight was timed to arrive at sunset. The bombers attacked the seven transports anchored in Davao Harbor, and met no resistance, enemy aircraft, or antiaircraft fire. Despite this, no hits occurred. Visibility was poor. The Fortresses landed at Del Monte after dark, and refueled.

Four, rearmed with bombs, departed Del Monte for Lingayen Bay 600 miles north. There they attacked transports of the invasion fleet in the bay. Visibility was again poor, and no hits were obtained. This time the B-17s met antiaircraft fire and enemy fighters. The antiaircraft barrage was ineffective but the fighters were so persistent that the bombers could not make a planned refueling stop at San Marcelino.

Instead, they flew directly to Australia. One B-17, low on fuel, landed at San Jose on Mindoro, an emergency strip. It refueled, and reached Australia safely. The other three B-17s landed at a Dutch airfield in Ambonia, refueled there, and returned to Darwin. The other five B-17s flew from Del Monte to Batchelor Field. All nine B-17s made the long flights without serious mechanical issues, testimony to the importance of adequate maintenance and spare parts.

A second strike against Davao left Batchelor Field on December 24. Three B-17s, each carrying 2,100 gallons of fuel and seven 300lb bombs departed. Two found the Davao airfield, and bombed at 15,000ft. The third attacked shipping in the harbor. This time they met opposition. All three returned safely to Darwin, but two were damaged. It would be the last time B-17s from Australia bombed Japanese targets in the Philippines.

MacArthur planned to stop the Japanese on the beaches at Lingayen. A combination of Japanese air power and US and Philippine Army weakness allowed the Japanese to get ashore, stay ashore, and quickly establish a beachhead. The Japanese spent their first two days at Lingayen consolidating their beachhead. US counterattacks against the Japanese went nowhere.

The logical next step for the US was to contain the Japanese on the beachhead, forcing Japan to conduct a frontal assault on prepared positions. That strategy collapsed however when the Japanese landed at Lamon – the beach was effectively undefended. US troops in South Luzon were failing to contain the force that landed at Legaspi on December 12. Most US units in central Luzon had been sent north in response to the Lingayen landing and there no ground troops to send to Lamon.

Japanese tactical bombers, many operating from airfields on Luzon, attacked retreating US forces. Their pressure transformed the retreat into a rout, and prevented the transfer of food, ammunition, and supplies from behind the Lingayen Bay beaches to Bataan. (AC)

The three Japanese landing beaches, Mauban, Atimonan, and Siain, were closer to Manila than Lingayen Bay was. The landings flanked the US lines around Lingayen, and also cut off the Philippine battalion sent to stop the Kimura Detachment at Legaspi. The only forces available for a counterattack were the remaining planes of the Interceptor Command: 12 P-40s and six P-35s armed with light bombs.

They strafed and bombed landing barges approaching the shore and attacked supply dumps already ashore. Flak was heavy. Two P-35s crash landed, other aircraft received damage, and though the attack offered personal satisfaction to the pilots surviving the attack, did little substantive damage. The landings continued unimpeded. It was a last gesture of defiance. All air force units received orders to abandon their Luzon airfields, and fall back on Bataan.

The order was given because it was impossible to continue holding the lines at Lingayen Bay. The road to Manila was open, whether from the north along the Luzon Plain from Lingayen to Manila or from the southeast over the Sierra Madre mountains. MacArthur decided to implement WPO-3, the prewar plan to evacuate Manila, move the Philippine government to Corregidor, and have the Army retreat to Bataan. Unfortunately, the supplies and ammunition previously stored at Bataan to support the prewar plan had been moved behind Lingayen Bay, to stop the anticipated invasion there.

The supplies and ammunition, painstakingly stockpiled behind the Lingayen beaches had to be abandoned. There were too few motor vehicles to move the supplies. The trucks which were available were attacked by Japanese warplanes if they moved during daylight hours.

The retreat, harried by Imperial Army aircraft, soon became a rout. The few units retaining cohesion, mostly those belonging to the US Philippine Division, fell back on Bataan. They were joined by those Philippine Army troops choosing to fight on, the ground echelon of the FEAF (including surviving members of the PAAC), and the remaining aircrew in Luzon, most of whom were without aircraft.

Over the next week, supplies were sent to Bataan from Manila, enough to feed 10,000 men for six months. This proved inadequate because by the time the withdrawal ended there were over 80,000 US personnel within the Bataan perimeter. Those who retreated to Bataan had time to prepare positions, because the Japanese, focused on capturing Manila, ignored those moving into Bataan.

MacArthur declared Manila an open city on December 26. This should have protected it from military attack, but the incoming Imperial Army fought its way into the city despite that. Civilian casualties were high and building damage extensive. (AC)

The US abandoned Manila on December 25. Military supplies, especially fuel which could not be moved to Corregidor or Bataan, was burned to deny it to the Japanese. Admiral Hart turned over all naval assets remaining in the Philippines to Admiral Francis Rockwell, who commanded the naval district. Hart left by submarine for Surabaya, to resume direct command of the Asiatic Fleet. General Brereton was ordered to move the FEAF headquarters south to Surabaya, and coordinate with Australia to keep lines of communications between Australia and Mindanao open. He departed for there on a Catalina on December 26, ultimately arriving at Darwin on December 29.

Manila was declared an open city on December 26. Tokyo acknowledged the declaration, and notified Homma. Word never filtered down to the Imperial Japanese Army Air Service or the ground troops. They continued attacking the city as if it remained a military target. Imperial air forces turned their attention to the Manila forts, bombing Corregidor for the first time on December 29. The Japanese army reached the gates of Manila on New Years Day, 1942. There they paused to consolidate, finally entering the city at dusk on January 2.

Japan spent three days restoring "peace and order" in Manila, a rough and ruthless process. Courts were suspended, the civil government remaining was put under "protective custody," and US and Commonwealth nationals rounded up and interned at Santo Tomas University. A bewildering set of regulations, permits, and licenses were implemented, with harsh penalties for violators, whether intentional or not. Civilians were warned that attempting to harm Japanese troops would be punished by death, with hostages taken and executed if perpetrators were not surrendered.

Ignorant of the army in Bataan, the Japanese assumed the conquest of the Philippines was complete and resistance had ended. They were wrong. It had not. Another five months of war remained.

## Endgame – January 6 to May 12, 1942

At first, Japan ignored US forces in Bataan, perhaps considering them unorganized and unimportant. From January 2 through January 8, while Japan was focused on Manila, US forces were conducting a fighting withdrawal into the Bataan Peninsula. Subic Bay, Olongapo, and Fort Wint were abandoned. By January 8 they held a defensive line anchored on Mount Natib, holding the southern two-thirds of the peninsula. Their rear was secured by the Manila Bay fortifications. Potential landing areas on Bataan's west coast were covered by reserve groups of troops. The terrain was such that had there been adequate reserves of food and ammunition, the US could have held out potentially indefinitely.

Nor was the US totally without air resources. Five airfields had been hastily built in Bataan in mid-December. Two were now behind Japanese lines, but three, Bataan Field, Cabcaben, and Mariveles, were within US lines. Most of the surviving US aircraft had been flown to them. Others were operating out of San Jose, an airfield expanded to military use after December 8 on Mindanao. Four damaged PBYs at Laguna del Bay were patched up and flown to Mindanao. They were now operating out of Lake Lanao, flying up to Corregidor and Mariveles Bay at night to bring supplies or carry passengers, departing before daybreak. The US continued to hold Del Monte, and a few other airfields in northwestern Mindanao.

To some extent, the US air forces would exist on sufferance for the next two months. The US

Japan occupied Clark Field as it advanced through the Luzon Plain. By February 1942 Japanese warplanes were flying out of Clark, and the Japanese were running their operations from the same room the US used when it held the base. During the war it became Japan's principal Philippine airfield. (AC)

air forces were scattered, Manila taken, and except for the Bataan Peninsula and Manila Bay's fortifications, the Japanese moved at will throughout the Philippines. Assuming this meant they had won, Japan withdrew most of the air units committed to the Philippines. Most of 5th Hikoshidan and the 21st and 23rd Koku Sentai were sent to support operations in Malaya and the Dutch East Indies after the fall of Manila. By then, Imperial Japanese aircraft were operating from captured US airfields. Clark Field became the major Japanese airfield in the Philippines.

Before departing, the 5th Hikoshidan and 11th Koku Kantai conducted a week-long aerial bombardment of Corregidor and the other island fortifications. It started on December 29, with an attack on Corregidor at 1230hrs by the 14th Sentai (with 18 Ki-21s), 8th Sentai (22 Ki-48s), and 16th Sentai (18 Ki-30s) escorted by 27 Ki-27s. This was immediately followed at 1300hrs by 60 G4Ms. Army Air Forces fighters in Bataan failed to intercept the attack that day, but antiaircraft fire from Corregidor was heavy and effective. Four dive-bombing Ki-30s were shot down. Several Ki-48s were damaged, with three shot down.

On January 2 the bombardment resumed. For the next five days Japan made daily raids. Fifty or more bombers participated, but only twin-engine bombers, Ki-21s, Ki-48s, and G4Ms. Dive bombers were excluded. The pattern was the same each day. A single aerial-reconnaissance flight occurred each morning. At 1230hrs, after the scout aircraft landed and its intelligence assessed, a formation of bombers arrived in a large V formation, flying over 20,000ft and above antiaircraft altitude. The large V broke up, and small formations of three to six aircraft made individual runs over the target. After two hours, all bombs were dropped, and by 1500hrs the bombers were flying home.

Corregidor was the main target, although on January 2 Fort Drum was also hit and on January 5 Fort Frank was a target. Surviving US fighters attempted to intercept a raid on January 4. Since fuel was short, the fighters did not take off until the approaching Japanese aircraft were reported. By the time the fighters were at altitude with the bombers, the bombers were already over the target, the attack was under way, and the fighters had little effect on the raid. They remained on the ground during subsequent raids, to conserve fuel.

The raids destroyed water and diesel storage tanks on Corregidor, destroyed Corregidor's electric railroad, repeatedly cut telephone cables (which were not buried deeply enough to be unaffected by bomb hits), and burned out anything flammable, including wooden buildings and their contents. Garrisons relocated from aboveground barracks to tunnels. The coastal batteries were undamaged. The exposed antiaircraft positions took hits, but damage was repaired quickly.

Except for nuisance raids, bombing Corregidor ceased thereafter until late March, as General Homma sent all but one fighter *chutai*, and his tactical bombers elsewhere after January 8. For the next three months Japanese air forces in the Philippines consisted of the Imperial Army's 10th Dokuritsu (independent) Hikotai with a *chutai* each of Ki-36s, Ki-51s, and Ki-15s, the Ki-27s of the 3rd Chutai of the 50th Sentai and 16th Sentai, and two sentai from the Imperial Navy.

The Japanese continued occupying new islands in the Philippines during this period, mostly to take airfields on those islands. They had taken Jolo on Christmas Day intending to use its airfield to support operations in Borneo. It was occupied by a battalion of Imperial Army infantry, two Imperial Navy Special Naval Landing Force battalions, and an Imperial Navy airfield construction unit.

The Japanese also landed on Mindoro in February. This was done to further isolate US forces on Bataan and Corregidor. The Japanese were so short of troops, they only held the north part of Mindoro, leaving the US airfield at San Jose alone, even though it was held by only 50 US airbase troops rather than infantrymen.

Before being transferred to assist the conquest of the Dutch East Indies, Ki-21s from the 5th Hikoshidan participated in a week-long bombardment of Corregidor. While it seriously damaged surface infrastructure (including buildings, fuel storage, and the railroad), it failed to damage subterranean facilities. (AC)

By mid-February the besiegers of Bataan, unknown to the besieged, were in a bad way. In addition to the aircraft, Japan had withdrawn one of its combat divisions, along with much of the armor. It had been replaced by a garrison brigade, filled by older men to conduct occupation duty, unsuited for the jungle warfare they were fighting.

None of the Japanese were really jungle fighters. Japan's Home Islands were in the temperate zone, with a climate more similar to the North American Pacific Northwest than the tropical Philippines. They were also short of supplies (although lavishly supplied when compared to the US in Bataan). Prewar, Japan planned to use Manila as their logistics depot, but because US Manila Bay fortifications blocked access to it, Lingayen Bay remained Japan's supply port. This required supplies to be trucked to Bataan on poor roads.

In late January and early February, the Japanese made several abortive attempts to flank the main line with landings well south of it. The US threw everything they could at the invaders, including the last flyable P-40s to strafe the landing barges. The US successfully contained and destroyed the invaders. By mid-February, combat, disease, and hunger had thinned out Japanese numbers to the point where the defenders outnumbered the attackers. Japan had exhausted itself taking half the peninsula originally held by the US. General Homma feared the US might launch a counterattack and rout his force.

Fortunately for Homma, US forces assumed they were outnumbered by the Japanese, though it was by then the other way around. Additionally, by February, the effects of short rations since reaching Bataan were being felt. Not enough food had been stored. Only a trickle came in by submarine and PBY, and only a trickle of personnel were leaving by submarines and PBY.

On the US side, it was not just the troops that were fading away. So were the remaining aircraft. However B-17s still flew the occasional bombing mission to the Philippines. Staging out of Malang on Java, they struck Japanese shipping in Davao

Imperial Army light bombers and dive bombers supported Imperial Army ground troops throughout the siege of Bataan. They served as mobile heavy artillery, clearing stubborn US positions. (AC)

Bay on January 5 and departing Kendari on Celebes they launched a second strike on January 11. A final B-17 strike against the Philippines hit Jolo on January 19. Thereafter, Japanese advances into Borneo and Sarawak turned the B-17s' attentions to Dutch East Indies targets.

Nor had the fighters on Bataan been totally quiet. On January 26–27 the surviving fighters there bombed and strafed Nielson and Nichols Fields, now occupied by the Japanese. The attack caused considerable damage. The two fields were scant minutes from Bataan, impossible for the Japanese to intercept before the attackers were already on the way home. Thereafter, and until the Japanese were sure no fighters remained, they based their aircraft at more distant bases, such as Iba, Clark, and Del Carmen Fields.

Minor US air operations from Bataan continued almost until it fell. On February 2, two P-40s strafed and bombed landing barges bringing troops to invade southern Bataan. On March 2, Bataan-based P-40s attacked Japanese shipping in Subic Bay, inflicting significant damage, but losing four P-40s. Some personnel evacuated to Australia by submarine. The only friendly aerial visitors were PBYs, stopping at Mariveles on taxi flights from Lake Lanao.

In December plans were laid to fly replacement P-40s and the A-24s to the Philippines from Australia in late January. Preparations started on December 28. This included training in long-distance flying cross-country and over water. From Brisbane they would fly to Darwin. From there they would island-hop across the Dutch East Indies stopping at Koepang, Makassar, Samarinda, and Tarakan. They would then cross the Celebes Sea to Malabang in Mindanao.

MacArthur was confident he could turn things around once they arrived. Rapid Japanese advances in Borneo (where Samarinda and Tarakan were), and the Christmas Day landing at Jolo blocked the transfers, especially after the Imperial Navy opened an airfield on Jolo in early January. The A-24s and P-40s were diverted to Java. The only aircraft capable of traveling between Australia and the Philippines were B-17s and PBYs operating out of Mindanao. Among those departing to Australia by air were Douglas MacArthur and his entourage. Ordered to leave the Philippines, MacArthur departed

Corregidor for Mindanao by PT boat on March 11. Accompanying him were his wife, son, his son's nanny, 13 Army and two Navy officers, and a technical sergeant. After arriving at Del Monte, they flew to Australia on three B-17s, two departing on March 17 and one on March 18.

A steady trickle of evacuees departed the Philippines aboard these bombers and the three remaining PBYs. Among those escaping to Australia by air were Philippine President Quezon and other senior members of the Philippine government, and men with knowledge critical to the continuation of the war, such as the PT officers, like John Bulkeley. The PBYs made a final one-way trip to Australia after a renewed Japanese air and ground offensive at Bataan made it impossible to make the Mariveles run.

By March, Japan's Imperial General Headquarters was becoming embarrassed by the lack of success in the Philippines. They sent reinforcements, both land and air. In the air, the 5th Hikoshidan 62nd Sentai returned accompanied by the 60th Sentai from the 3rd Hikoshidan. Both flew Ki-21s, 60 in all. The Imperial Navy sent two bomber Hikotai totaling 24 G4Ms, one fighter Hikotai with 12 A6Ms, and a Kokutai of single-engine carrier bombers. They began arriving in mid-March, operating out of Clark Field.

The aerial assault on Corregidor began March 24 and continued for the next four days. Imperial Army bombers left Clark Field at dawn. Five Army *chutai* were followed by the two Imperial Navy G4M *chutai*. At 0924hrs Corregidor's air raid siren sounded, followed a minute later by bombs dropping. Each *chutai* bombed in turn, nine-aircraft formations, dropping 250kg and 500kg bombs. They attacked from 22,000–28,000ft, above US antiaircraft fire and untroubled by US fighters.

The unopposed attacks were made in a leisurely manner. Each bomber dropped its bombs deliberately to maximize accuracy. As one formation finished, the next followed. When the 45 Army Ki-21s were done, the 24 Navy G4Ms took over. When the main attack ended, three-aircraft formations continued attacking Corregidor at intervals. These attacks continued into the night. In all 71 tons of bombs hit Corregidor that day.

Del Monte surrendered after the fall of Corregidor, as ordered by General Wainwright. After the surrender, Japanese troops occupying the airfield posed by P-40s abandoned on the airfield. (AC)

The next day the Imperial Army returned with only three *chutai*, 27 Ki-21s. The Imperial Navy again sent 24 G4Ms. Except for fewer Army bombers, the previous day's pattern was repeated. A massive and deliberately conducted initial bombardment was followed by small nuisance raids every two to three hours for the rest of the day and night. This continued until March 29.

On March 29 and from then until April 1 the Imperial Army sent only two *chutai* of Ki-21 to Corregidor, although the round-the-clock bombing continued. While the G4Ms continued attacking Corregidor, the rest of the Imperial aircraft shifted to Bataan, to support a new ground offensive. Ki-21s struck the rear areas, disrupting communications and supplies. The single-engine attack, bomber, and fighter aircraft struck the front lines, serving as airborne artillery.

The final Japanese offensive against Bataan began on April 3 and culminated with a US surrender on April 9, 1942. Imperial Army aircraft were active throughout the advance, flying 150 sorties the first day. It continued its support until the Japanese achieved victory, contributing materially to the Imperial Army's ultimate ground victory. Several thousand US Army and Navy personnel were evacuated to Corregidor before Bataan surrendered. This included General Jonathan Wainwright, who had taken command of US forces in the Philippines after MacArthur's departure.

The surviving fighters at Bataan flew to Del Monte, strafing Japanese targets during this flight. Once at Del Monte, they provided air cover for B-17s staging to Del Monte from Australia. Between April 8 and April 12, B-17s flying out of Del Monte struck targets at Japanese forces in Legaspi, Cebu, Iloilo, and Davao. Then the B-17 departed Mindanao forever. The P-40s continued operating until May 1, when Japanese forces on Mindanao finally overran Del Monte.

After Bataan, it was the Corregidor's turn. It took another month to take Corregidor. Aerial bombardment played a less important role in that action. Heavy artillery was available, could reach Corregidor from Bataan, and was cheaper and more accurate than airstrikes. Corregidor fell after a nighttime invasion on May 5. The garrison surrendered the next day. Among the prisoners was General Wainwright. He attempted to surrender just the Corregidor garrison, but the Japanese continued attacking until he agreed to surrender all US forces in the Philippines. Thereafter, organized resistance on the Philippines ended.

# AFTERMATH AND ANALYSIS

The US sent too many obsolete or inadequate aircraft to the Philippines in 1940 and 1941. The B-18 was being phased out in favor of more modern medium bombers even as B-18s were being sent. When war finally came, surviving B-18s were relegated to flying spare parts from Nichols Field to Del Monte. (NMAF)

With the surrender of all US forces the Japanese believed they had finally conquered the Philippines. From a conventional military standpoint they succeeded. MacArthur, now commanding Allied forces from Australia, had pledged "I shall return," but in 1942 the road back to the Philippines from Australia seemed long and difficult, a goal perhaps impossible to achieve.

As US General James Mattis observed later, in a similar context, in war "the enemy always gets a vote." In this case, some US soldiers, American and Filipino, voted to continue the battle. They melted into the mountains and jungles, either to sit out the war or to conduct a guerilla insurgency against the Japanese. Small at first, it grew throughout the rest of the war. Escaped prisoners of war and alienated civilians joined the insurgency. Supplies and support were sent from Australia. Allied forces redeemed MacArthur's promise, returning to the Philippines in November 1944, almost three years after the war opened. By then, Filipino guerillas controlled significant chunks of Mindanao and other Philippine islands.

Homma, the campaign's victor, was felt to have mishandled the campaign. Imperial General Headquarters never used him in another active role, forcing Homma into retirement in 1943. Postwar, he was tried for atrocities committed after the surrender of Bataan. Of the 60,000 POWs taken, over 6,500 died on the march to Japanese prison camps, in what became known as the Bataan Death March. He was convicted and executed.

MacArthur, whose decisions led to an abject collapse of the US forces in the Philippines, took command of Allied forces in Australia. His miserable performance in the Philippines proved the nadir of his career. He eventually became the senior US Army commander in the Pacific Theater, accepting the surrender of the Japanese at Tokyo Bay in September 1945.

Postwar he became military governor of Japan, and commander of US forces in the Far East during the Korean War. He demonstrated that some of those who fail go on to have outstanding careers afterwards. While not as brilliant a general as his acolytes claimed, he was not as wretched as his detractors assert.

Over one-tenth of those surrendering at Bataan died marching to prison camps. It became known as the Bataan Death March. While the total numbers surrendering was unexpectedly high, it did not relieve Japan of its obligation to treat prisoners humanely. (AC)

The air forces in the campaign moved on to different campaigns and different fates. The 5th Hikoshidan moved to Malaya, Thailand, and the Dutch East Indies, where it became part of Japan's 3rd Kokugun (Air Army), headquartered in Singapore. The hikoshidan's units spent the rest of the Pacific War there, defending the oilfields and refineries around that area and supporting operations in Burma. Placed in what became a relative backwater, but one needing air cover, it survived relatively intact through the first quarter of 1944. Then the increasing strengths of the Allied air forces ground it to pieces.

The 11th Koku Kantai went south. It became involved in the struggles for New Guinea, New Britain, New Ireland, and the Solomon Islands. Initially it participated in their conquest, continuing to provide long-range air support for amphibious operations and ground offensives. Later, they participated in the defense of those islands, most notably in the struggle for the Solomons and Rabaul. By summer 1944, shorn of most its aircraft, it was reduced to conducting the same type of nuisance raids on US forces that US fighters on Bataan made against the Japanese in 1942. It finally surrendered at Rabaul when the war ended in August 1945.

The Far East Air Force was reorganized as the V Air Force. Commanded by General George Kenney, it led MacArthur's march back to the Philippines. Along the way it amassed an enviable string of victories and an impressive record of tactical innovation. They proved deadly to Japanese land, naval, and air units. The first numbered air force created outside the continental United States, at war's end it remained in the Far East, headquartered in Japan, where it remains today. It saw combat in the Korean and Vietnam Wars, and saw service in the Cold War and 21st century War on Terrorism.

Many Far East Air Force veterans went on to have a distinguished World War II service. Lewis Brereton was reassigned to North Africa. He organized the Ploesti low-level mission in 1943, and went on to command the IX Air Force and First Allied Airborne Army. Major Emmett "Rosie" O'Donnell as a Brigadier General commanded the first B-29 strike against Tokyo on November 24, 1944. He remained in service postwar in what became the US Air Force, with a combat command in Korea, and retiring as a full general in 1963. Paul "Pappy" Gunn, a civilian airline pilot in the Philippines when the war started was directly commissioned into the Army Air Forces. In 1942 he developed the gun-armed B-25s and A-20s that proved deadly against Japanese ships.

The 11th Koku Kantai left the Philippines a triumphant victor. Yet in 1944 it would be ground to dust attempting to hold Rabaul. Many of the bombers which attacked Clark Field and Cavite ended up as derelicts at Rabaul. (AC)

The Japanese air forces however were clearly the victors in this campaign. Two questions worth exploring are why did they win so handily, and could the US have won?

A big reason for Japan's comparatively easy victory lay in the combat philosophies of the air forces of the two nations. Japan's air forces, Imperial Army and Imperial Navy, were purely tactical organizations, designed to support the surface combatants for the service to which they belonged. Both served their parent organizations, as indicated by their names: Imperial Japanese Army Air Service and Imperial Japanese Navy Air Service.

Imperial Army air doctrine was straightforward: capture advance airfields to bring your aircraft near the troops they are supporting; suppress enemy aircraft so they could not attack your troops or ships; provide direct ground support to troops in the field, serving as airborne artillery; make it difficult, if not impossible for enemy ships to safely operate in waters you wish to control. Imperial Navy air doctrine differed only in the range it was to operate. Their aircraft had much longer range than Imperial Army aircraft to allow the Imperial Navy to project power over oceanic distances.

This doctrine fit a campaign like this perfectly. Initial landings on each island captured airfields to bring aircraft within minutes of the troops they were intended to support. The follow-up main landings could operate under a friendly air umbrella. That US ground forces were inept made the race to Manila look easy, but without air cover it is possible that the US aircraft might have pinned Japanese troops on the beach until even the undertrained Philippine Army could have dealt with them.

The differences between the Imperial Army and Navy air doctrine proved complementary. Imperial Army aircraft concentrated on direct support of the Imperial Army. Imperial Navy aircraft, with their greater range concentrated exclusively on the enemy's deep rear. It knocked out the FEAF airfields and the US Navy installations which could have offered resistance, destroying the FEAF and chasing the US Navy out of the Philippines.

The Japanese performance lacked brilliance. They missed the significance of the US retreat to Bataan during the Japanese race to Manila. This allowed the campaign to run for another five months. It was workmanlike, honed by nearly four years' experience

By the time Japan invaded the Philippines, long experience had honed Japan's ability to launch combined service amphibious operations. Their pattern was grabbing an airfield at a lightly defended spot near their objective, moving warplanes there, and using them to provide air cover over the main invasion site. (AC)

conducting combined amphibious operations in China. Bataan did not alter the outcome of the campaign, merely delayed it.

By contrast, US air efforts were unfocused. The US Army Air Forces were more interested in proving strategic bombardment could win wars than on providing air cover and support for troops on the ground or ships at sea. Unlike the Royal Air Force, they had a tactical support role for the Army Air Forces. That A-24s were heading to the Philippines demonstrated a commitment to ground support, yet the leaders at the USAAF were too heavily invested in strategic bombardment – so much so that they sent most of the then-available B-17s to the Philippines.

There was no real doctrine associated with B-17s for tactical airpower. These were aircraft designed to operate from high altitude against distant industrial targets, but in the Philippines they would be defending against invasion. Their targets would be small and agile: ships, tanks, and troop formations, better suited to being attacked by the A-24s that never arrived. Possibly they were envisioned for use against Japanese airfields and harbors in Formosa; large, stationary targets against which a B-17 formation would be effective.

Yet while plans were drawn up prewar to attack Formosa, MacArthur considered them as provocative and the idea of prewar reconnaissance flights over Formosa even more provocative. Even after war began it took General Brereton nearly a full day to receive permission to conduct a photoreconnaissance mission. A strike mission to Formosa would take place still later, perhaps the next day.

Given this lack of readiness, it is easy to conclude that the US hoped the presence of a large concentration of heavy bombers in the Philippines would intimidate Japan into avoiding war. Instead, it provided Japan with a priority target for the attack they were already determined to make.

Prewar US disposition of aircraft demonstrated further unpreparedness. While squadrons were dispersed to alternate fields, the dispersal fields were permanent airfields north of Manila. Every airfield as far south as Manila was within easy reach of Formosa-based Japanese aircraft. Since the US had no intention of launching a preemptive strike, it should have assumed any war would begin with a Japanese strike and positioned its air assets out of reach of the Japanese.

It started this with the heavy bombers, building Del Monte in Mindanao and stationing half the B-17s there prewar. It had airfields south of Manila where it could have stationed its fighter squadrons, Batangas, Legaspi, and San Jose (in Mindanao) among them. Only the US Navy took the threat seriously enough to position most of its major units outside the range of Japanese aircraft and to locate half of its air search assets outside their permanent bases at Olongapo and Cavite.

US commanders seriously underestimated both the chances of war and Japanese capabilities. Part of this was due to the magical thinking then prevalent at MacArthur's headquarters. It based war plans on unrealistic assessments of the untrained Philippine Army's abilities. Part of it was due to racial prejudice. This thinking was representative of most US military attitudes towards Japan. The Japanese were viewed as weak, myopic, and incompetent. In this campaign this belief proved fatal.

One fascinating aspect of this campaign was its scale. Relatively few aircraft were involved on either side. On paper, the two sides were relatively even, with the US having 307 aircraft in the Philippines and the Japanese committing 443 warplanes to the Philippine expedition. Had the war started a month later it would have been even. Another 126 aircraft (36 B-17s, 36 A-24s and 54 P-40s) were in transit to the Philippines when war broke out, and these were superior to the Japanese bombers and Imperial Army fighters committed.

Yet perhaps 100 of the US aircraft were obsolete (B-10s and P-26s), observation aircraft, or simply unflyable (including half the P-35s), and the massacre of US aircraft on December 8 precluded any kind of an even fight. Japan secured air superiority on December 8 and air supremacy by December 10.

Yet even the largest Japanese raids on the opening days were small by standards of 1944 and 1945 when hundreds of aircraft were committed to a single raid and thousands of aircraft flew multiple sorties during air battles. Even by the standards of the Battle of Britain they were small. No more than 54 bombers and a similar number of fighters conducted raids on individual airfields on December 8 and 10.

Could the United States air forces have prevailed in the Philippines? Theoretically they could have. With a realistic assessment of US ground strength (including the Philippine Army) a more rational land campaign could have been crafted around holding Bataan. With available reserves of ammunition, supplies, and food stored there, a picked 50,000-man force could have held out for over a year. Aircraft operating from fighter fields within Bataan and Mindoro supported by B-17s operating out of Del Monte could have prevented Japanese aerial support from being effective. At a minimum it would have disjointed Japanese timetables.

MacArthur was not a counterpuncher and this is a counterpunching strategy. It required aircraft initially to have been withdrawn out of range of Formosa and a defensive stance on the ground. Instead, MacArthur committed to an all-out offensive to crush the Japanese on the beaches.

## Surviving aircraft

Few examples remain of the aircraft that fought in the Philippines in 1941–42. The types present were obsolescent types being phased out, such as the Japanese Ki-15 or US P-26, or were early versions of aircraft types used throughout the war. Examples of those include the Ki-15-1a and B-17C/D. Most of these early-war types were destroyed over the four years of war that followed or were discarded immediately after the war ended, with more modern aircraft being retained.

There appear to be no intact surviving examples of the Japanese Ki-15, Ki-21, Ki-30, Ki-51, and Imperial Navy G3M, much less any in flyable condition. There are two K-27s, three Ki-48s, three G4Ms which survive today, in whole or part. All surviving Ki-27s

"The Swoose" was a veteran of the 1941 Philippine campaign, flying to Australia in December 1941. It is the last surviving B-17D, and is currently undergoing restoration at the National Museum of the Air Force in Dayton, Ohio. (NMAF)

and Ki-48s are intact and on static display at different museums. Only one G4M is complete, displayed unrestored at the Planes of Fame Air Museum. It left the factory about the time the Philippines campaign ended. The other two are partial restorations or combinations of different G4Ms. All are G4M1s, the model flown in the Philippines, but none were present.

There are 30-odd surviving Mitsubishi Zeros. Many are of uncertain provenance, a few assembled from bits and pieces of multiple wrecks or with a large number of replica parts. Several are later model Zeros, built after the conquest of the Philippines. There appear to be no surviving Japanese aircraft which participated in the campaign.

A similar situation exists with US aircraft. No A-27s survive. All were destroyed in December 1941. There is one B-10 and six B-18s still around, all in various air museums in the United States. None were in the Philippines. Two P-26s still exist, one in flyable condition. Neither was in the Philippines. A replica P-26 in PAAC colors is on display at Bataan.

Multiple examples of the PBY, P-40 and B-17 survive today; over 100 PBYs (including foreign variants), 85 P-40s, and 45 B-17s are still around. The vast majority of these are late model versions of these aircraft. No PBY1 through PBY4, the types flown in the Philippines, survive today. All are PBY5 or later versions. Of the P-40s still around, only one is a P-40B and only 14 are P-40Es, the two types flown in the Philippines. Three P-40Es are flyable. None served in the Philippines in 1941–42, but they are identical to the types which flew there.

Of the B-17s, there is one surviving B-17D, representative of the B-17s operating out of Clark and Del Monte Fields. It is a veteran of the Philippine campaign. Then known as "Ole Betsy," it arrived in the Philippines in September 1941, and fought there in December 1941 and January 1942. In January, it was flown to Australia, rebuilt, and renamed "The Swoose." Converted to an executive transport, it was scheduled to be scrapped in 1946 but one of its pilots, Olympic diver, USAAF aviator, and Clark Field survivor, Frank Kurtz, convinced the City of Los Angeles to preserve it as a war memorial. Later donated to the Air Force, it is now being restored for display.

# FURTHER READING

For this book, my most important sources were official histories and chronologies. On the US side those of the US Army, the US Army Air Forces, and the quasi-official Morison US Navy History. On the Japanese side, I relied most heavily on *Japanese Operations in the Southwest Pacific Area*, assembled postwar by US interviews with Japanese officers. I filled these out with memoirs of participants. These have to be treated with care, because those writing the memoirs have imperfect knowledge and are frequently trying to spin a performance that was less than satisfactory. Yet they are valid.

I also used some unit histories, works like Francillon's excellent history of Imperial Japanese aircraft, and miscellaneous other minor sources, including orders of battles for the two sides. Not all of these are listed due to space considerations.

Through the grace of Abebooks.com I was also able to secure (at a reasonable price) a copy of a 1943 Japanese publication, *Philippine Expeditionary Force*. This provided a wealth of pictorial information from the Japanese side of the conflict. It offers a little-seen side of the campaign. It largely writes the Imperial Navy out of the script, leading me to conclude it may have had an Imperial Army sponsor.

Books marked with an * at the end are available online, for those interested.

AAF Historical Office, *Army Air Forces in the War Against Japan, 1941–1942*, Headquarters Army Air Forces, Washington, D.C., 1945*

Brereton, Lewis H., *The Brereton Diaries: War in the Air in the Pacific, Middle East and Europe, 3 October 1941–8 May 1945*, William Morrow and Company, New York, 1946*

Craven, Wesley Frank and Cate, James Lea (eds), *The Army Air Forces in World War II, Volume One, Plans and Early Operations, January 1939 to August 1942*, Office of Air Force History, Washington, D.C., 1983*

Edmons, Walter D., *They Fought With What They Had: The Story of the Army Air Forces in the Southwest Pacific, 1941–42*, Little, Brown, and Company, Boston, 1951*

**TO FILIPINOS IN DAVAO**

The Japanese Forces have already landed. They have come to free you and all your brethren in the Philippines. Japan is not fighting the Philippines but only America so give the Americans no cooperation. They are your real enemies. We are your friends. Do not mistreat Japanese in Davao for they are your best friends. Japanese Forces will give Filipinos every consideration, but if you harm the local Japanese in any way, the punishment will be severe.

**ANY HARM DONE TO JAPANESE RESIDENTS WILL BE DEALT WITH SEVERELY.**

A propaganda leaflet distributed in Mindanao in an attempt to persuade Filipinos to support Japan Many Filipinos remained hostile to the Japanese. Many initially neutral about Japan shifted to hostility due to Japanese behavior. (NMAF)

Francillon, Rene J., *Japanese Aircraft of the Pacific War*, Funk & Wagnalls, New York, NY, 1970

MacArthur, Douglas, *Reports of General MacArthur, prepared by his General Staff, Volume I*, US Government Printing Office, Washington, D.C., 1966*

MacArthur, Douglas, *Reports of General MacArthur: Japanese Operations in the Southwest Pacific Area, Volume II, Part I*, Government Printing Office, Washington, D.C., 1994*

Messimer, Dwight R., *In the Hands of Fate: The Story of Patrol Wing Ten, 8 December 1941—11 May 1942*, Naval Institute Press, Annapolis, MD, 1985

Morison, Samuel Eliot, *History of United States Naval Operations in World War II, Volume 3: The Rising Sun in the Pacific*, Little, Brown, and Company, Boston, 1946

Morton, Louis, *United States Army in World War II: The Fall of the Philippines*, Center of Military History, United States Army, Washington, D.C., 1993*

Villamor, Jesus A., *They Never Surrendered: A True Story of Resistance in World War II*, Vera-Reyes, Quezon City, Philippines, 1982

# INDEX

Figures in bold refer to illustrations and tables.